MINIA
SCHNAUZI
THE MINIATURE
SCHNAUZER

Miniature Schnauzer Total Guide

MINIATURE SCHNAUZERS: MINIATURE SCHNAUZER PUPPIES, MINIATURE SCHNAUZER TRAINING, MINIATURE SCHNAUZER SIZE, HEALTH, & MORE!

Mark Manfield

© DYM Worldwide Publishers

Published by DYM Worldwide Publishers, 2018.

ISBN: 978-1-911355-73-1

DYM Worldwide Publishers takes no responsibility for, and will not be liable for, the websites being temporary or being removed from the Internet. The accuracy and completeness of the information provided herein, and opinions stated herein are not guaranteed or warranted to produce any particular results, and the advice or strategies, contained herein may not be suitable for every individual. The author, publisher, distributors, and/or affiliates shall not be liable for any loss incurred as a consequence of the use and application, directly or indirectly of any information presented in this work. This publication is designed to provide information regarding the subject matter covered. The information included in this book has been compiled to give an overview of the topics covered. The information contained in this book has been compiled to provide an overview of the subject. It is not intended as medical advice and should not be construed as such. For a firm diagnosis of any medical conditions, you should consult a doctor or veterinarian (as related to animal health). The writer, publisher, distributors, and/or affiliates of this work are not responsible for any damages or negative consequences following any of the treatments or methods highlighted in this book.

Website links are for informational purposes only and should not be seen as a personal endorsement; the same applies to any products or services mentioned in this work. The reader should also be aware that although the web links included were correct at the time of writing they may become out of date in the future. Any pricing or currency exchange rate information was accurate at the time of writing but may become out of date in the future. The Author, Publisher, distributors, and/or affiliates assume no responsibility for pricing and currency exchange rates mentioned within this work.

Table of Contents

CHAPTER 1

Introducing the Miniature Schnauzer

Spunky and dapper, the Miniature Schnauzer is a dog breed that has turned its cheerful, sociable personality into a consistent appearance on the list of the most popular dog breeds in the United States, Canada, and throughout Europe. Truly "man's best friend," this little fella is an energetic extrovert, a loyal sidekick, and a wonderful addition to the family. The walrus mustache may make the Mini Schnauzer look sophisticated and intellectual, but he is really affectionate and comical. The Miniature Schnauzer is smart, active, curious, and loving...all in one fun-sized package!

The mini-Schnauzer dog breed likes to defy stereotypes. For example, you might think that his tiny stature means the Miniature Schnauzer is a perfect lap dog, but in fact, the breed requires a lot of exercise and, despite being affectionate, he can sometimes be standoffish. Cuddles happen on his terms. But rest assured, he has "his terms" a lot so there will be plenty of cuddles with your Mini Schnauzer. This dog breed is also very protective of his family, so the feisty, little Miniature Schnauzer can, despite his small size, be an excellent guard dog. He will bark at suspicious strangers as if to say, "No way! Not on my watch!"

The comical mustache is a hallmark of the Mini Schnauzer.

The goal of this Miniature Schnauzer book is to help you discover if the Mini Schnauzer is the right dog breed for you, and to learn more about your new Miniature Schnauzer puppy if you decide the answer to the first question is "yes." This fun-loving breed offers plenty of unique benefits to pet owners, but you should be aware of some breed-specific information of the dog breed Schnauzer and mini Schnauzer, and issues so that you can keep your dog happy and healthy. In this miniature Schnauzer handbook, you will read about how to find a reputable breeder, how to introduce your Miniature Schnauzer to your household, how to feed your new pet, and how to keep him fit and healthy. You will also learn about caring for Miniature Schnauzers during each stage of life, from the carefree puppy days through the golden years.

This Mini Schnauzer book will also help you if you decide to breed your Miniature Schnauzer or show your dog. In fact, the Miniature Schnauzer is the subject of some debates in the dog show circles, and you will gain an understanding of these controversies. The more you know about this well-loved breed, and the more you increase your miniature Schnauzer savvy, the more you can appreciate the special attributes and characteristics that have helped move the Miniature Schnauzer up the ranks of popular dog breeds, and into so many people's hearts.

CHAPTER 2

History of the Miniature Schnauzer

Today's Miniature Schnauzers are primarily used as companion dogs, but their initial purpose was to work. What were Schnauzers bred for? This breed served an important function on the farms of Germany, where the breed originated. German farmers wanted a tenacious and diminutive dog to rid the farmhouses, barns, and outbuildings of rats and other vermin. Infestations of rats posed serious problems to rural people living 150 to 200 years ago. Rats carried disease, ate stored foods, and destroyed crops. To eradicate the rodents, German dog breeders crossed the Standard Schnauzer, also known as the German Schnauzer, with black poodles and Affenpinschers to develop a dog that was similar in appearance and disposition to the Standard Schnauzer, or black Schnauzer dog, but smaller. They created a small dog they dubbed the ZwergSchnauzer, which translates to "dwarf Schnauzer." We know it as the Miniature German Schnauzer, wirehaired Schnauzer, or the miniature Schnauzer terrier, but most commonly just the Miniature Schnauzer.

The Miniature Schnauzer can trace his family tree back to the farmlands of Germany.

The Schnauzer in Medieval Europe

The Schnauzer dog breed as a whole was developed in Western Europe during the medieval era by breeding for favorable traits, including his herding and ratting ability and good guard dog behavior. They were a staple on German farms for centuries, but German dog breeders began to pay attention to them when dog shows became popular in the 1800s. It was during this time that breeders started to breed the dog to a specific standard and temperament. Before the establishment of clear breed standards and breed specific clubs, litter mates could be classified as different breeds -- either short-haired German Pinschers or long-coated Schnauzers -- depending on the appearance of the puppy's coat. Although some of the original German Pinscher coat types were most likely lost during World War I, the grey, or salt-and-pepper colored coat that is typically seen on the North American Standard Schnauzer, as well as the German Pincher, or silberpinsch, remains strong and serves as a visual link between the two closely-related breeds.

The Mini Schnauzer is the smallest of the three types of Schnauzers… the Miniature Schnauzer, the Standard Schnauzer, and the Giant Schnauzer.

The Development of the Miniature Schnauzer

How the name Schnauzer was even given to this breed, and its full-sized counterpart is an interesting story. The development of the Miniature Schnauzer occurred much later in history than some other dog breeds, although specific records and dates have been lost to time. We do know that, in 1879, a mustached wire-haired pinscher named Schnauzer, won first place at a dog show in Hannover, Germany. In the German language, the word "Schnauzer" means mustache, so the dog was aptly named. So much so, in fact, that the entire breed became known the Schnauzer.

A true Miniature Schnauzer dog named Findel was the first documented miniature version of the Standard Schnauzer breed when her birth was recorded in October of 1888. Just seven years later, the first breed club for Miniature Schnauzers was founded in the German city of Cologne, although the records show that other dog breeds were included in the club. At this time, the Miniature Schnauzer and the Affenpinscher were often viewed as the same breed of dog, but by the early 1900s, the two were recognized as separate breeds.

Miniature Schnauzer Coat Colors

During the early days of the Mini Schnauzer, the little dog was bred to have a variety of coat colors, from russet red to straw yellow to black and tan combos. Preferences have evolved and, today, we see the little dogs primarily in salt and pepper grey, solid black, black and silver, or solid grey.

The Miniature Schnauzer During World War I

When World War I broke out in Europe, dog breeding took a backseat to the war effort. Many dog breeds were nearly lost during these years, but not the Miniature Schnauzer. The scrappy little dog breed was so popular among American soldiers fighting in the first Great War that many of them took Miniature Schnauzer puppies back home with them when they returned to the United States. This introduced the Miniature Schnauzer to a whole new continent of dog lovers.

In 1926, just a few years after the breed was first brought to the United States, the American Kennel Club recognized the Miniature Schnauzer as a distinct breed. By August of 1933, the American Miniature Schnauzer Club was established in response to the increased number of Miniature Schnauzers in America. Today, the Miniature Schnauzer is in the top twenty most popular dog breeds, according to the American Kennel Club…a position it has easily maintained for several years.

The Curious Classification of the Mini Schnauzer

One curious thing about the AKC's classification of the Miniature Schnauzer, however, is that the breed is categorized as a terrier. It is shown in the terrier class. The Standard Schnauzer, from which it was created, though, is found in the Working Group. This discrepancy is an indicator of the differences in appearance and temperament between the Standard Schnauzer and the Miniature Schnauzer, as we detail in the next chapter.

CHAPTER 3

What are the Breed Standards for the Miniature Schnauzer?

The Miniature Schnauzer is the most popular of the three Schnauzer breeds, the Standard Schnauzer, Giant Schnauzer, and Miniature Schnauzer, but it differs greatly in size and coloring from the other two. The Miniature Schnauzer is between 12 and 14 inches (30.48 to 35.56 centimeters) tall and weighs between 11 and 20 pounds (4.98 and 9.07 kilograms). By comparison, the Standard Schnauzer height is 17 to 20 inches (43.18 to 50.8 centimeters), and the full-grown miniature Schnauzer weighs between 30 and 58 pounds (13.60 and 26.30 kilograms). The Giant Schnauzer size is considerably larger. The Giant Schnauzer's weight is between 55 and 80 pounds (24.94 and 36.28 kilograms) and is typically between 24 and 29 inches (60.94 and 73.55 centimeters) in height. Although some dog breeders will market their puppies as Toy Miniature Schnauzers or Teacup Miniature Schnauzers, these are just terms being used to describe a regular Miniature Schnauzer. The breeders may assign the adjectives of toy or teacup to a Miniature Schnauzer puppy that is on the smaller size of the standard size range, or even below the average size, but

Toy Schnauzers and Teacup Schnauzers are not separate breeds. When researching Miniature Schnauzer breeders, be sure to question claims of micro teacup Mini Schnauzers, micro Mini Schnauzers, or teacup Mini Schnauzers to make sure the puppy is a purebred Schnauzer, and not mixed with a toy breed of another dog.

Spunky little Miniature Schnauzers weigh between 11 and 20 pounds (4.98 and 9.07 kilograms).

What are the Recognized Miniature Schnauzer Coat Colors?

Black and salt-and-pepper grey are the only two accepted colors of the coats of the Giant Schnauzer and the Standard Schnauzer. However, there is more variety with the Miniature Schnauzer. Black Miniature Schnauzers, white Miniature Schnauzers, black and silver Miniature Schnauzers, and salt-and-pepper Miniature

Schnauzers (or grey miniature Schnauzer) are all accepted by the German breed club standards. However, in the United States, Australia, and Canada, the white Miniature Schnauzer is not a recognized or accepted color, and in Britain, neither the white Schnauzer nor the black-and-silver Schnauzer is recognized.

What are Parti Miniature Schnauzers?

Miniature Schnauzer puppies, however, can be born with different colored coats. Called Parti Miniature Schnauzers, these dogs boast a patterned coat and are the subject of a bit of controversy among Miniature Schnauzer fanciers. To fully understand this debate, we need to go back to the latter years of the 19th century.

When the Pinscher-Schnauzer Klub of Germany, the PSK, first published its first breed standards in 1880, it listed a parti-color of white with black patches among its acceptable coat colors. This inclusion showed that Schnauzers with black and white patches occurred during this time period, although these Schnauzer puppies were not widely popular. No parti color Schnauzers were registered in this first breed standard book.

Fast forward to September 4, 1929, to Countess v. Kantiz's kennel in Podangen, Germany, where a litter of black Miniature Schnauzer puppies was born. Mysteriously, three of these puppies had black and white parti coats. The Countess, an avid breeder of Mini Schnauzer puppies, kept meticulous records and could trace the lineage of these puppies back six generations, proving that all of these puppies' ancestors were black Mini Schnauzers. The Countess bred these parti puppies and produced the second generation of six black and white parti Mini Schnauzers.

Parti Schnauzers can have brown, tan, wheat or white coats.

Countess Kantiz's parti Schnauzers became the first parti puppies registered and officially recognized by the Pinscher-Schnauzer Klub in Germany, but a few years later, in 1933, the members of the board of the PSK voted to ban parti Schnauzers from future registration. Numerous Schnauzer breeders and dog experts of the day petitioned the Klub to reverse its decision and allow for the acceptance of Parti Schnauzers. Despite the fact that Countess Kantiz could prove that her black and white parti Miniature Schnauzers were purebred back the required three generations, the Klub denied their request and upheld its ban on parti Schnauzers.

The Countess was distraught to hear this. She believed that the decision was economically motivated. Germany was experiencing an economic depression in the first half of the 1930s, and dog breeders were producing more Schnauzer dogs than could be sold. Adding to this, the wire-haired Fox Terrier was enjoying a boost in popularity, particularly in Britain. The PSK board members felt that the parti Miniature Schnauzer was too close in appearance to the Fox Terrier and that the similarities would cause confusion between the two dog breeds that would lead to a decrease in sales for Mini Schnauzers. Countess Kantiz argued that the parti dogs remained purely Schnauzer and any claims that they were crossed with Fox Terriers was unfounded. She proposed a compromise.

The Pinscher-Schnauzer Klub of Germany conceded to Countess Kantiz and agreed to create a separate and distinctive breed for the parti Schnauzers. These plans were derailed, however, when World War II broke out, and the case of the parti mini Schnauzers was not revisited. Even today, black miniature Schnauzer puppies born with patches of white are denied entry into breed clubs in Germany, and across the globe.

Although you cannot show a Miniature Schnauzer that bears a non-standard coloring, Miniature Schnauzer colors can be varied: white Miniature Schnauzers, chocolate or liver Mini Schnauzers, Silver Miniature Schnauzers, Platinum Mini Schnauzers, and wheaten or tan Miniature Schnauzers.

What is the Miniature Schnauzer Breed Description?

Today the American Kennel Club, or AKC, describes the Miniature Schnauzer as an active dog that closely resembles the Standard Schnauzer from which it was developed. Like all Schnauzer dogs, the Mini Schnauzer has a blunt, rectangle-shaped head with a flat skull and unwrinkled forehead. The Mini Schnauzer has small, oval-shaped, dark brown eyes that are expressive and show his curiosity and intelligence. When left uncropped, the ears of the Miniature Schnauzer breed are V-shaped and lie close to the head. The Mini Schnauzer dog has a strong, arched neck and with the skin fitting snugly over the throat of the animal.

The Mini Schnauzer's body is small and compact with straight, paralleled front legs. The back end of the dog should be muscular with slanted thighs. The belly of the Miniature Schnauzer should not appear to be pulled up at the flank. A Miniature Schnauzer has small, rounded paws with thick, tough pads of black skin. Miniature Schnauzers carried their tails high and erect, though the tails are often docked just long enough to show beyond the body line. Like the Standard Schnauzer dog and the Giant Schnauzer dog, the Miniature Schnauzer has a double coat. The outer coat is stiff and wiry while the undercoat is smooth and close to the body.

CHAPTER 4

Is the Miniature Schnauzer the Right Dog for Me?

Before you commit to making a Miniature Schnauzer part of your life, you should explore the breed to determine if the Mini Schnauzer is the right dog for you. When you understand the Miniature Schnauzer temperament and personality, as well as the requirements of the breed, you can decide if you can provide the best home life for this breed of dog.

Because it is a great family dog, the Mini Schnauzer remains one of the most popular dog breeds.

What is the Miniature Schnauzer Temperament?

Energetic, curious, smart, and spunky are all terms often used to describe the Miniature Schnauzer personality. The Mini Schnauzer may be small in stature, but he is big on personality. He doesn't seem to realize he is small; he believes he is the alpha, but he is friendly and outgoing, rather than aggressive. This dog breed is protective of his home and his family and will bark to alert you to potential threats…or what he perceives to be potential threats, like the mail carrier or the trash truck. The Mini Schnauzer temperament is ideally suited for apartment dwellers as well as for those living in rural areas with wide, open spaces. This little dog can easily adapt to his surroundings. In fact, adaptability is part of the Schnauzer personality. So is trainability. The Mini Schnauzer is a quick learner and exceptionally bright.

You will be amazed and impressed by his intelligence. He may be smart, but he is also a bit of a clown. He is easily amused and loves to get into mischief of his own making. He is inquisitive and likes to explore his surroundings, and he is clever enough to figure out how to open cabinet doors and maybe even to the door to the outside! An independent little dog, he just might let himself outside.

What are the Miniature Schnauzer Space Requirements?

The Miniature Schnauzer can quickly adjust to his surroundings. This breed is well-suited for those living in apartments or small houses. The Mini Schnauzer is a somewhat energetic dog, however, so if you lack a yard, you will probably need to take your pup for daily walks to burn off his energy and help him stay fit and healthy. If you live in a rural area or on a farm, the Miniature Schnauzer breed is perfect for you, too. He is hardy and a sturdy little guy who won't easily tire if he is out patrolling the property. The Schnauzer breed is used to work, and your dog will be happy to help guard your home.

Will the Miniature Schnauzer Like My Family?

Yes! The Miniature Schnauzer and your family is the perfect combination. The Schnauzer breed, in general, is a great companion dog, and the Mini Schnauzer is especially so. The spunky little dog will get along famously with all members of your family, but he sometimes plays favorites. The Mini Schnauzer will often pick one family member and bond with that human more than the rest. He is affectionate to all, but from time to time, he will want to be left alone. He will cuddle you, but on his own terms.

Will the Miniature Schnauzer Get Along with My Children?

Generally speaking, the Miniature Schnauzer is a great family dog and is friendly towards children. However, you should always supervise all interactions with any dog and children to avoid injuries to the youngsters and to the dog. Mini Schnauzers were bred to be good companion dogs and have an easy-going temperament. If they are socialized with kids, from the puppy stage on up, and if the youngsters are taught to be kind and respectful of the dog…you will most likely end up with a fabulous family dog that will love and protect your kids. The Mini Schnauzer loves to run and play and will have endless days of fun playing with your children. The Mini Schnauzer breed is rugged and sturdy so it can handle a bit of playful roughhousing.

Miniature Schnauzers adapt easily to other pets in the house.

Will the Miniature Schnauzer Get Along with My Other Pets?

Because the Mini Schnauzer has been bred and developed to be a farm dog, it is accustomed to living alongside other animals. They generally adapt quickly to sharing their home with another dog or with cats and get along fine with them. Your Miniature Schnauzer is curious and playful and likes to amuse himself so he may find it funny to chase the cat around or annoy your other dog. Remember, he is not doing this to be mean or aggressive. He is simply amusing himself. As a breed, the Miniature Schnauzer was developed as a ratting dog to help hunt rats and other vermin on the farms of rural Germany. It is in their make-up to go after these pests. Your little Schnauzer may not understand the difference between an invading mouse and your pet hamster. Always supervise your pets when they interact and be mindful of the Schnauzer's instincts, when you let your hamster or gerbil out of its cage.

Does the Miniature Schnauzer Demand a lot of Attention?

The Miniature Schnauzer attention requirements vary from dog to dog, but in general, the breed is outgoing but independent. There may be times with your Mini Schnauzer acts aloof, but when he wants some attention, you will know it. He will demand that you stop what you are doing and shower him with love. In fact, they thrive on affection and attention, but that attention doesn't have to be pets and cuddles. It could be playing catch or tug-o-war in the yard or going for a long walk in the park. Because of their natural curiosity, your Miniature Schnauzer dog will want to know what you are doing at all times and will follow you around the house, trying to join you in all your activities.

What Are the Miniature Schnauzer Grooming Requirements?

When compared to other dog breeds, the Miniature Schnauzer doesn't shed very much. Because they shed very little, the coat can get matted if it is not regularly brushed. It is an easy task, though. The Mini Schnauzers love to be brushed and groomed and will politely sit while you brush through their coat, soaking in the attention. You may need to take your pooch to a groomer occasionally to be trimmed and pampered, but in general, the Miniature Schnauzer is not a high-maintenance breed.

CHAPTER 5

How Do I Find a Miniature Schnauzer Puppy?

Sure, you can do a Google search and find Mini Schnauzer puppies for sale in your area, but how do you know they are coming from a responsible breeder and not a puppy mill? First, you should have a working knowledge of how reputable breeders operate their facility. Second, you should know what to ask and what to look for.

A responsible Miniature Schnauzer breeder will guarantee a healthy pup.

How Do I Find a Reputable Miniature Schnauzer Breeder?

Before you contact a Miniature Schnauzer breeder that you have found online or through your veterinarian, develop a list of questions for the breeder. Don't feel as though you are over-cautious or annoying; a responsible dog breeder will happily answer your questions because they want to make sure they are placing their animals in good homes. In fact, a good breeder will probably have a lot of questions for you, too. They will ask about your living arrangements and family and lifestyle. They aren't nosey…they want to see if the puppy is a good fit for you. Be prepared to answer all their questions honestly and openly.

Do a Phone Interview with the Breeder

Even before you go to the breeder's facility to see the cute little Miniature Schnauzer puppies, call the breeder and discuss their puppies over the phone. Don't rely on texting and email for this. A lot of information can be gained by hearing their voice. You should ask them some basic questions, such as how long have they been breeding Mini Schnauzers and why they chose to breed this particular dog breed. Also, ask if the puppies' parents are on site and available for you to meet and if they offer a health guarantee. Also ask about veterinarian visits, vaccinations, and de-worming of the puppies. A competent breeder will be able to answer these questions easily. The reason why you should ask these questions in a telephone interview, and not on-site, is that it removes the emotional aspect of the process. When you are at the breeder's kennel, surrounded by cute Mini Schnauzer puppies, it will be difficult to concentrate on the breeder's answers. And it will be even harder to leave without a puppy! You may become so emotionally vested and hypnotized by the puppy cuteness, that you end up with a puppy that doesn't meet your requirements. Remember that cuteness doesn't equal quality.

Visit the Breeder's Kennel

Use your visit to the breeder's kennel to do a quick evaluation. Is it clean? Are the animals well-cared for? Where are the Mini Schnauzers being kept? Are there any animals that look sick? Try to keep the conversation with the breeder focused on their breeding operation, and feel free to ask questions. Be prepared to walk away if you aren't satisfied with the answers you are getting.

Watch how the puppies interact with each other. They should all be playful and friendly. Try sitting down on the floor with them and let them come to you. Don't select the bully or the alpha puppy that seems pushy and aggressive, but also don't pick the quiet and shy one that acts scared and timid. Pick up a few puppies and make sure they are used to being handled. Look in their eyes to see if they are clear and bright. Snap your fingers to test the hearing of the puppies.

The responsible breeder will give you plenty of time to pick out a puppy. Once you do, he or she will ask you to read and sign a breeder's contract. The contract will discuss the breeder's guarantee of the animal's health and information about the puppy's medical history. You should also receive information about the purebred registration application process, diet and puppy care, and pedigree papers.

You may not be able to bring your puppy home right away. A respectable Mini Schnauzer breeder will not relinquish a puppy until it is seven or eight weeks old, is fully weaned and eating solid food, has been vaccinated, and socialized.

How Do I Find a Miniature Schnauzer Rescue Organization?

A dog rescue organization is a non-profit group, usually run by volunteers, that works to save lost, injured, or abandoned dogs. Although there are general rescue groups, there are also breed specific groups, dedicated to re-homing that particular breed, like the Miniature Schnauzer. There are irresponsible pet owners who no longer want their dog when it grows out of the puppy stage or people who can no longer care for their pet because of changes to their lifestyles, finances, or health. Often times, these animals end up in a shelter or pound, and then to a rescue group.

Most Miniature Schnauzers that end up in rescue organizations are older than one year. Older dogs should not be ruled out or written off. They need and deserve love, too, and, in many cases, they are well-behaved and trained, having left the puppy stage behind them.

Because the rescue groups are non-profit organizations, they operate on donations. If you find the Mini Schnauzer you want through a rescue group, expect that they will charge you an adoption fee to offset the costs of their work. Rescue dogs are spayed or neutered and vaccinated.

Like Mini Schnauzer breeders, Miniature Schnauzer rescue organizations are dedicated to the breed. Knowing that many unwanted dogs are euthanized, they are committed to stopping this practice by placing wonderful purebred Schnauzers with loving families.

CHAPTER 6

What Should I Know About Miniature Schnauzer Puppy Mills?

There are responsible Miniature Schnauzer breeders and then there are people and businesses involved in the irresponsible breeding of Mini Schnauzers. When you are looking around for Miniature Schnauzers for sale, it is important to identify a reputable breeder – one who is knowledgeable about the Miniature Schnauzer breed and is dedicated to producing top quality dogs – versus a questionable breeder – one who is more concerned about making money than they with the health of the puppies. In this chapter, we take a look Mini Schnauzer puppy mills so you can make an informed decision when looking for a new, little furry companion.

To avoid heartache, look for a reputable dog breeder who puts the quality of the breed ahead of making money.

Backyard Breeders versus True Puppy Mills

When you answer a Schnauzer for sale ad, keep in mind that there are casual backyard breeders and then there are true puppy mills. A backyard breeder is probably someone who owns one or more Miniature Schnauzers as pets. They, then, decide to breed two of their Mini Schnauzers, or breed one of their dogs with a friend's Mini Schnauzer to sell the puppies. Although backyard breeders may love the Mini Schnauzer breed, they are most likely not as knowledgeable about breed standards and how to breed for temperament or to enhance specific traits. Puppies born to backyard breeders may be acceptable pet-quality dogs, but they also may have some genetic problems. They may be friendly and playful, but you may find yourself with unexpected veterinarian costs later in the animal's life.

Then there are the true puppy mills. A puppy mill is categorized as a dog breeding operation that is more focused on making a profit than on the welfare of the animals. Often, the dogs are kept in filthy and crowded conditions and are not given adequate care and socialization. Puppy mills do a number of things to maximize their profits, such as selling puppies that are younger than eight weeks old, selling unvaccinated puppies, and breeding the females as soon as they can, with no time to recover from the previous litter.

Puppy mill breeders do not focus on producing genetically superior Miniature Schnauzers or other breeds of dogs. In fact, they have no concerns about the genetic quality of the animals they produce. As a result, the Mini Schnauzers that come from puppy mills are prone to congenital disorders and abnormalities, such as respiratory diseases, epilepsy, and structural defects.

Puppy mill dogs are sold to the naïve and unsuspecting owner through ads for Miniature Schnauzer puppies for sale, in the newspaper or on the internet. If you answer one of these ads and they suggest meeting you somewhere other than the kennel where the puppy was born, this is a red flag that it is a puppy mill facility. A reputable Mini Schnauzer breeder would welcome you to their kennel, and invite you to meet the puppy's parents. They want you to see the cleanliness of the kennel and how well-cared-for the Schnauzer puppies are. The puppy mill owner, on the contrary, wants to hide the fact that there are multiple litters of puppies at their facility, that the dogs are kept in crowded cages, that the conditions are unsanitary, and that parasites and diseases run rampant.

Pet Stores

Pet stores often acquire their dogs from puppy mill breeders. According to the Humane Society of the United States, 99% of the puppies in pet stores originate in puppy mills, despite what the pet store employees tell you. Reputable Miniature Schnauzer dog breeders won't take their puppies to pet stores to be sold because it is a violation of the ethics code of nearly all of the national dog breed clubs. Also, responsible Mini Schnauzer breeders are concerned about the well-being of their puppies; therefore they want to meet the buyers, so they are assured that their pups are going to a good and loving home. Investigations conducted by the Humane Society of the United States, have shown that some of the breeders who supply animals to pet stores have a history of multiple violations of the Federal Animal Welfare Act.

When shopping for a new Mini Schnauzer puppy to welcome into your family, be on the lookout for some red flags that you may be dealing with a puppy mill owner. If the owner tries to sell you a Miniature Schnauzer puppy that is younger than eight weeks, it may be because he is just trying to move out his merchandise as quickly as possible. Also, if the pup isn't vaccinated and has not yet seen a veterinarian, it may be a sign that the breeder is trying to cut costs, by foregoing routine medical visits. When you meet the puppy, observe to see if he is clean and active and playful. If he seems shy, quiet, and reserved, those are signs that he had not been socialized, or has endured some stress or trauma. Lastly, a reputable dog breeder will be able to give you a pedigree showing the lineage and health history several generations back, typically three to five generations.

If you suspect you are dealing with a puppy mill operator, you should walk away, no matter how cute the Mini Schnauzer puppy may be. If you do business with a puppy mill, you are supporting this type of business, and contributing to its continuation. If every puppy buyer refused to purchase from a puppy mill facility or from pet stores that supply them, the practice would eventually die out. You will also be helping the Miniature Schnauzer breed as a whole, because responsible breeders act as caretakers of the breed, ensuring genetic quality and overall health.

CHAPTER 7

How Do I Prepare to Bring My New Miniature Schnauzer Home?

B efore you bring your new little bundle of love home, you need to make sure that you, your family, and your house are all ready to welcome you new Miniature Schnauzer. Much like bringing home a newborn human baby, the more prepared you are for the big day, the happier your Mini Schnauzer puppy will be…and the less stressed you would be as well! In this chapter, we will discuss the puppy supplies that you need to have on hand before you open your home to a new Schnauzer puppy, as well as the steps you need to take to safely puppy-proof your home. In addition, we will discuss ways to make the transition into your family a smooth and stress-free one.

*Prepare your home ahead of time for the arrival
of your new Miniature Schnauzer pup.*

How Do I Puppy-Proof My Home?

Well before you welcome your tail-wagging furbaby home,
be sure your house is ready. Allow yourself enough time to
thoroughly puppy-proof your home to make sure that your
Miniature Schnauzer puppy will stay safe and healthy. This
requires being alert to dangers that may be present at his level.
To do this, get down on your hands and knees and survey the
land from your puppy's point of view. In doing so, you will notice
things you may not have seen before, such as stray items left
under the couch or cords dangling from the mini blinds.

In the kitchen, make sure that the cupboard doors shut securely. If they don't, your Mini Schnauzer puppy may be able to nose open the cupboard and help himself to what is inside. The same is true for kitchen drawers. The clever and curious little Miniature Schnauzer may quickly learn how to get into drawers too. You could consider installing child safety locks on all the lower cupboard doors and drawers to ensure that your puppy can't get a hold of something that is potentially dangerous or poisonous, such as the cleaning supplies you store under your kitchen sink.

Thoroughly puppy-proof the bathrooms, too, as these rooms can house hazards for an inquisitive puppy. Make sure your family members don't miss the trash can when throwing away cotton swabs, cardboard toilet paper tubes, hair ties, disposable razors, or the tiny plastic caps to toothpaste tubes and shampoo bottles. All of these things present choking dangers to your Miniature Schnauzer puppy. Encourage all family members to put the toilet seat down after use. A tiny puppy may jump up on the toilet and fall in…or try to drink from the toilet bowl.

Mini Schnauzer puppies have a keen sense of smell and are attracted to items that smell like you. Remember this, when you leave clothes, socks, slippers, shoes, and more lying on your bedroom floor. It is like an invitation to start chewing. It is for this same reason that your Miniature Schnauzer puppy might decide to chew on your eyeglasses, hearing aid, or wristwatch. Not only can these items cause injury to your puppy if eaten, but they are costly to replace. Always keep these items out of reach, and in a safe location.

Throughout the house, keep power cords, phone chargers, earbuds, and extension cords away from your puppy, as much as you possibly can. For the cords you can't eliminate, you can run them through PVC piping so the curious little Mini Schnauzer can't chew on them. Beyond that, be diligent about keeping items off the floor and reducing clutter. That goes for your child's toys, throw pillows, coasters, and magazines, too.

If your home has stairs, you may need to get a baby gate to keep your Mini Schnauzer puppy from taking a tumble down the steps.

What Supplies Do I Need to Have on Hand?

Be sure to have all the supplies you need already at your house when your Mini Schnauzer arrives. You don't want to leave your puppy alone so soon after you welcome him home because you need to run to the store for some item you forgot. You will have more bonding and play time while your puppy makes himself at home if you get everything you need before the big day.

You need to have food and water dishes for your new best friend. Every pet store sells individual stainless steel food and water bowls, or you can purchase a single dish that has two bowls built in. Whichever one you chose, make sure it is tip proof. Puppies can get rambunctious and excited when they are eating or drinking…or just playing around…and will spill over their bowl many times if they are given a chance. Another option is an automatic feeder and waterer that continuously fills your puppy's food and water.

Pick out a good collar, harness, and leash, before your puppy comes home. A harness is recommended when using a leash. The dog may strain against the leash, and a harness will protect his neck and throat. The collar is useful for identification tags. You will probably also want to purchase an identification tag with your contact information on it, in case your Mini Schnauzer puppy runs off. The collar should be made of soft fabric so it is comfortable and doesn't chafe. It shouldn't be too snug or too loose. If you can easily slip two fingers underneath the collar, then it is a good fit. The small size typically works well for a Miniature Schnauzer collar, and you can upgrade to the medium size as your puppy grows. You should plan on keeping your puppy on a leash when you take him outside so be sure that you purchased a leash when you picked up the rest of your puppy supplies. Either a nylon or leather leash will work for your Miniature Schnauzer. You can even select a retractable leash, so you can control the dog's range when you are out for a walk.

Your new puppy needs a cozy bed.

43

Be sure to have a dog crate with a nice, soft dog bed all set up and ready for your new Miniature Schnauzer. Either a wire or plastic crate will work. Inside the crate, add in bedding material that is washable and absorbent, but also durable and not easily destroyed by chewing. You will need to wash the bedding often to keep it clean and dry. You can also put a dog bed in the crate for added comfort. Soon, your Mini Schnauzer puppy will become accustomed to his crate and will view it as his safe place. Dog beds that have bumper sides or side walls can provide a cozy, enclosed feeling for your Schnauzer dog. Do not get a bed that is too large or your dog won't feel as snug and warm; the more comfortable it is, the better.

Your new puppy will want to play, so be sure to have some Miniature Schnauzer toys on hand from day one. Although there are not specific Mini Schnauzer toys, any top quality dog or puppy toy designed for smaller dogs will work. Look for puppy toys that cannot be easily torn apart and without small pieces that the Schnauzer dog can choke on. You should aim for offering a variety of toys, keeping in mind that if your Mini Schnauzer puppy is entertained, he is less likely to chew on your shoes, laptop charger, or your daughter's beloved teddy bear.

When you pick up your new Miniature Schnauzer from the breeder, find out what kind of puppy food they have been feeding him, and if possible buy that brand and formula. You will soon be able to introduce the puppy food of your choice, but you will want to introduce it slowly by mixing it with the food he is used to. This way, your Mini Schnauzer won't experience tummy distress. You can also ask the breeder for a gallon jug of the water that the puppy is used to drinking. Sometimes unfamiliar water tastes different, and a puppy won't drink it. If you use the breeder's water for the first few days, it reduces the number of changes that your puppy will have to face, all at once. While it may be tempting to purchase a bunch of puppy treats, don't spoil your new Mini Schnauzer puppy too much. Treats can be too rich for the Mini Schnauzer puppy's tender little tummy.

Although you will most likely not need to groom your puppy right away, it may be a good idea to have Miniature Schnauzer grooming supplies at the ready. This includes a brush for unmatting his coat and a good, quality dog shampoo for puppy baths. Look for a shampoo that is mild and free of chemicals and additives that may be too strong for baby's tender skin. You will have plenty of time later to purchase Schnauzer clippers, Schnauzer grooming brushes, and other Miniature Schnauzer grooming tools, once the puppy gets his full coat, which will be around six or seven months of age.

CHAPTER 8

What Should I Feed My Miniature Schnauzer?

With all the commercial dog foods on the market today, it is hard to know what you should feed your Miniature Schnauzer. You know, of course, that nutrition is important for the proper growth of your Mini Schnauzer puppy and to maintain the health of your older Miniature Schnauzer dog. In this chapter, we will review Miniature Schnauzer food and nutritional requirements, Schnauzer puppy food, adult Schnauzer nutritional needs, and more. We will also discuss the pros and cons of dry dog food, canned food, and homemade dog food, and provide you with a list of foods your Miniature Schnauzer should avoid.

Proper nutrition is vital to keeping your Miniature Schnauzer healthy.

Adult Miniature Schnauzer Feeding

Mini Schnauzers are active, high-energy dogs, so they need to eat a diet that helps fuel their busy lives. A good Miniature Schnauzer dog food has sufficient protein and calorie content. Smaller dog breeds, such as the Miniature Schnauzer, burn more calories per pound than mid-sized and large breed dogs, so they need to consume more calories proportionally for their body weight. On the contrary, their smaller stomachs won't allow them to gorge themselves. This means the adult Mini Schnauzer needs food that is more nutrient dense with higher calorie content than typical dog food. Many dog foods developed for small breed dogs will meet this requirement.

Full grown Miniature Schnauzers weigh, on average, about 15 pounds. To maintain this weight, an active Mini Schnauzer should consume roughly 532 calories per day. A young adult Mini Schnauzer that is more active may need as much as 620 daily calories, while older, less active, and spayed or neutered dogs require less than the 532 amount.

Often times, a Mini Schnauzer will nibble and graze at his food dish all day long, if you leave the bowl sitting out all day. Knowing that he has food at his will, he will snack throughout the day, rather than eating a full meal. The grazing habit may lead to overeating, and your Mini Schnauzer may pack on a few extra pounds as a result. Instead of providing your dog with a constant food source, try measuring out the correct amount of food into his food bowl and allow him access to it for a shorter period of time, perhaps half an hour. This should be plenty of time for your hungry Mini Schnauzer to eat his fill. After that time, put the bowl away. Adult Miniature Schnauzer should eat two meals per day. This gives them time to digest each meal through their tiny digestive systems while ensuring that they meet their calorie intake for the day.

Miniature Schnauzer Puppy Feeding

Mini Schnauzer puppies have different nutritional needs to help them grow strong and healthy. The food that your puppy eats should be higher in calories and protein, and more chock full of nutrients than adult dog food. The bellies of Mini Schnauzer pups can be delicate things, so be consistent with the food you offer to your Schnauzer baby. Changing the brands of puppy food can cause gastronomical distress for your puppy, leading to vomiting and diarrhea, and maybe even allergies.

Puppies are much more active and expend more calories as they play and run, as compared to adult dogs. Commercial dog food that is formulated for small breed puppies should be able to meet the needs of your growing puppy. You can give your Mini Schnauzer puppy three meals a day as their feeding schedule, until they are old enough to switch to adult food.

Miniature Schnauzer puppies need food with the proper balance of calcium and phosphorus. In fact, the ratio of calcium to phosphorus is 1.2 parts calcium to 1 part phosphorus. The amount of calcium is vital to bone growth for the little puppy. When selecting a puppy food, always read the nutritional information that is printed on the label.

Senior Miniature Schnauzer Feeding

The average life expectancy of the Miniature Schnauzer ranges from 12 to 15 years, but the dog enters his golden years at around 9 years old. As your Mini Schnauzer ages, his dietary needs change. Older dogs become less active, so they don't need as many daily calories as more active adult dogs. If you don't alter his calorie intake, your aging Schnauzer may start to put on weight. An overweight dog is prone to a variety of health problems such as arthritis and diabetes; therefore you should take steps to prevent obesity. Some commercial dog food brands have developed special blends for senior dogs so you can decrease your Schnauzer dog's calorie intake without feeding him less.

What are the Connections between Miniature Schnauzer Health Problems and Diet?

For the most part, Miniature Schnauzers are a healthy dog breed. Some health issues, however, can crop up that can be directly contributed to the diet the dog eats. Eating a diet that is too high in fat can lead to conditions such as pancreatitis and hyperlipidemia. Avoid adding extra fat to your Mini Schnauzer's diets by not giving him table scraps to prevent this.

What are the Nutritional Requirements for Miniature Schnauzers?

When choosing dog food for your Mini Schnauzer, make sure that you look at the nutritional analysis information that is listed on the side panel of the package. The Miniature Schnauzer fat requirement should be 10 to 15%.

Your dog needs an adequate amount of protein as well as ensure proper growth and development. An adult Mini Schnauzer should get at least ten percent of their calories from protein. More important than the amount of protein is the quality of it. It is possible for one brand of dog food to contain all protein from rabbit meat, while another may reach the same percentage of protein by combining chicken meal, soybean meal, and grains. All proteins are not created equal, and your Mini Schnauzer's body will digest each type differently. Knowing the quality of the protein in your dog's food, and its source will help you make sure you are feeding your precious puppy the best food you can.

The Miniature Schnauzer diet should contain at least fifty percent carbohydrates and between 2.5 and 4.5 percent of fiber.

Plant material, such as rice, barley, and oats, should comprise the Miniature Schnauzer carb requirements. Wheat products many cause allergies and skin problems in Mini Schnauzers and should be avoided.

Is Dry Dog Food or Canned Dog Food Better for My Miniature Schnauzer?

Commercial dog food comes in either dry form or in cans in wet form. But which is best for your Miniature Schnauzer? Consider the pros and cons of each.

Miniature Schnauzer dry food, or kibbles, is more convenient and easy to store. You can more easily measure out the correct amount of food with kibbles. It can be safer for your Mini Schnauzer, too, because you can leave it out in your dog's bowl all day long without fear of it spoiling. Lastly, kibbles tend to be less costly than canned food.

Miniature Schnauzer canned food is wetter and can be, therefore, an additional source of hydration for your pet. Wet dog food is also a good choice for older Schnauzers or ones who are ill or missing teeth. Some dogs lose their appetite as they age and pet owners find it difficult to coax them to eat. Canned dog food is more flavorful and has a stronger odor than kibbles, so dogs are more inclined to eat it.

Canned dog food is more prone to spoilage and must be refrigerated after opening. It is less convenient to measure out the correct amount for your dog, and it can create more waste. It is also, typically, more expensive than dry dog food.

Nutritionally speaking, it is possible to find high-quality food for your Miniature Schnauzer in both canned form and kibbles. The choice between the two really comes down to your own personal preference. Consistency is important, though. Pick one and stick with it as much as possible. Switching back and forth between kibbles and cans will disrupt your Mini Schnauzer's delicate system.

What Should I Know about Homemade Dog Food?

You may think that homemade dog food is a better option for your Miniature Schnauzer, but before you commit the time, energy, and cost that comes with producing homemade dog food, there are several things to consider. The first, and most important, question to ask yourself is, do you think you can make food for your Mini Schnauzer that is equal to or superior to the commercial dog food that is on the market? The majority of the quality dog foods has been designed by scientists, researchers, veterinarians, and dog nutritionists to make sure the product meets the nutritional requirements of the Mini Schnauzer. Can you do better than them?

Producing Miniature Schnauzer homemade dog food that is nutritionally sound is more difficult than it sounds. It is also a lot of work, time-consuming, and costly. If you are committed to the process, though, you may be able to take more control over your Mini Schnauzer's diet.

The first step is to find a good recipe. Not all recipes are created equal, so you should ask your veterinarian or pet nutritionist for suggestions and guidance. They may be able to point you towards recipes that have been developed by scientists and nutritionists to meet the specific requirements of the Mini Schnauzer. The recipe will include a source of protein, typically animal meat or eggs, carbohydrates from vegetables and grains, and some fat, such as oil. You also need to include calcium, such dairy, and essential fatty acids, that can be found in egg yolks, oatmeal, and specific plant oils.

To ensure that you maintain all the nutrients, you must prepare the recipe exactly as stated, not altering the directions or substituting ingredients. Use a food scale so you can accurately measure your individual ingredients. You should also make sure that you thoroughly cook the meat to kill bacteria, but also cook the grains and vegetables. They are easier for your Miniature Schnauzer to digest after they have been cooked.

If you decide to offer your Miniature Schnauzer homemade food, be sure to let your veterinarian know, and keep the lines of communication between you and your vet open. It would probably be a good idea to take your Mini Schnauzer in for a vet visit a few weeks after starting him on a homemade dog food diet. If your dog has gained or lost weight, it may mean that the diet needs to be adjusted. Your vet can also tell if your dog's diet is satisfactory by examining his coat, skin, teeth, and eyes. Based on this information, you and your vet can make decisions about your dog's diet.

Can I Give My Miniature Schnauzer Treats?

Absolutely! You can reward your Mini Schnauzer for mastering tricks or spoil him for being cute with a doggie treat. Just remember that moderation is the key. Too many treats will fill your Miniature Schnauzer's belly with empty calories and ruin his appetite for his dinner. Additionally, too many treats can upset your dog's tummy. Just as you did when choosing a top quality dog food for your Mini Schnauzer, do your research on doggie treats and purchase the ones you feel are best for your dog. Read the ingredients and avoid treats with fillers and artificial ingredients. You can also give occasional treats of fresh foods, including green beans, pumpkin, and peanut butter.

What Foods Should My Miniature Schnauzer Avoid?

Foods to avoid for Miniature Schnauzers include items that pose a choking hazard and items that are indigestible or poisonous. The main choking hazard in Mini Schnauzers comes from bones. You should refrain from giving your Miniature Schnauzer any kind of bones. Bones can splinter or break apart and lodge in the animal's esophagus or in the intestinal tract, causing a blockage and tissue damage.

Some foods that are perfectly fine for humans to eat can be toxic to Miniature Schnauzers. Dark chocolate can cause trouble in the Mini Schnauzer's nervous system, causing seizures and death. Garlic, chives, and onions all contain a substance that can inhibit the production of red blood cells, leading to anemia in the dogs. Walnuts can turn toxic and will make your Mini Schnauzer very ill. Likewise, Macadamia nuts can produce body tremors and vomiting in dogs. Miniature Schnauzers should not consume the pits from fruits either, as many of these contain cyanide which can kill a small dog. Do not allow your pet to drink coffee, tea, soft drinks, or alcoholic beverages. Many other foods that we humans find delicious can be poisonous to your Miniature

Schnauzer. As a general rule of thumb, avoid giving your pet human food unless you are sure that it is safe, and when you are certain, only in small amounts.

A vegan Mini Schnauzer?

Can I Feed My Miniature Schnauzer a Vegan or Gluten-Free Diet?

So many people are taking control of their food choices and adopting diets that make them feel healthy and energized. These include vegetarian and vegan diets, as well as gluten-free diets. For pet owners who are dedicated to their food choices, it may be tempting to extend your dietary beliefs onto your dog. But is it safe for your Miniature Schnauzer?

Like all dogs, Miniature Schnauzers are technically carnivores. This basic fact of biology can put a vegan or vegetarian regime at odds with their biology. How can they ensure that their pet is receiving a satisfactory diet that is based on animal meat when they are morally opposed to killing and eating animals? Given a choice, a dog will always choose to eat meat over plants, but the dogs will eat some plant-based foods. While cats are true carnivores, dogs are also able to extract their nutrients from plant sources. Throughout the thousands of years of dog domestication, dogs have adapted to eat a starch diet. This remains one of the biggest biological differences between domesticated dogs and their wolf cousins.

When you start your Mini Schnauzer on a vegan or vegetarian diet, keep in mind that his digestive system is vastly different from yours. Don't assume that what works for you will work for your Miniature Schnauzer. Discuss your dietary restrictions and concerns with your veterinarian or pet nutritionist and follow their advice. Together, you can develop a feeding plan for your Mini Schnauzer that will provide your dog with the protein and nutrients he needs, while heeding your ethical concerns.

Gluten is a wheat enzyme that causes allergic reactions and digestive issues in many humans. Dogs, too, can experience allergies – often manifested in skin disorders – from consuming wheat gluten. Luckily, it is easy to avoid gluten. Many commercial dog foods are gluten-free. Instead of relying on wheat proteins, these products use cereal grains and rice, which are easier for your dog to digest.

CHAPTER 9

How Can I Train My Miniature Schnauzer?

Miniature Schnauzers are intelligent creatures who learn quickly and want to please their owners. This means they are highly trainable. You will want to start training your Mini Schnauzer puppy as soon as you bring him home, so he learns from the very beginning that you are the pack leader, and he is to be obedient to you. Training your Mini Schnauzer takes some consistency and patience, but soon, you will have a well-behaved little fella that respects you…and your carpets…and is a pleasure to have as a member of your family. Your Miniature Schnauzer training will be threefold: basic life skills, correcting negative behavior, and doing tricks. We will discuss all three aspects of training in this chapter.

*Miniature Schnauzers are intelligent little
dogs and love to learn new tricks.*

Basic Life Skills Training

Your Mini Schnauzer needs to learn a few house rules when he begins his life with you and your family. His first lesson should be in Mini Schnauzer housetraining. Whether you opt to use puppy pads or newspaper is a matter of personal preference. Honestly, your puppy doesn't care where he does his business. He may even forego the puppy pads or newspaper altogether, and soil your carpet or furniture if you don't watch out. You will have to keep a close eye on him and whisk him outside or to the newspaper if you see him strike that familiar pose. As you are moving him, repeat a specific command, such as "outside" or "potty time." Soon your Miniature Schnauzer puppy will come to associate the act with the command. Mini Schnauzer housetraining will go more easily if you keep your dog on a consistent feeding and potty schedule. Even with a set schedule, your Miniature Schnauzer may need to relieve himself at random times throughout the day. Be attuned to his body language and his attempts to communicate. He may yip at the door, asking to go out, or he may paw at his puppy pads.

If you will be leaving your Miniature Schnauzer puppy alone at home while you are at work all day, or if he is often destructively mischievous, you may want to crate train him. Like housetraining, Miniature Schnauzer crate training is most effective when it is consistent and regularly used. Although some dog owners feel as though dog crates are cruel, they actually provide a safe haven for your pet. The crate should be viewed as your Miniature Schnauzer's personal bedroom. It should have his soft and welcoming bed in it, as well as a few of your pet's favorite toys. It may be tempting to use the crate as a type of doggie jail when your pup misbehaves, but your dog should not come to associate his crate with being punished. You may find that your Mini Schnauzer goes into his crate on his own when he is tired or overwhelmed. When not used solely as a form of punishment, the crate transforms into your dog's safe place when he needs some alone time. And also like housetraining, you should use a command word when you place your Mini Schnauzer in his crate, such as "crate" or "cage." Pretty soon, he will run to his crate, when he hears the command.

Miniature Schnauzer leash training is also important. After all, you want to be able to take your pup on walks or to events with you. But you also want to make sure he knows how to behave when on the leash. An untrained Mini Schnauzer puppy will pull at the leash and strain against it which is why it is recommended that you attach the leash to a harness, rather than a collar. You should begin leash training as soon as your puppy settles into his new home. Don't wait until the first time you need to take him somewhere. He should get used to the feel of the leash and learn his limitations at an early age. Let him run around inside wearing his collar, harness, and leash so he can get used to how it feels. All the time, you should be playing with him so he begins to associate leash time with fun. You can introduce a command when you use the leash, so your Mini Schnauzer understands what is coming. Some dog owners use word commands, such as "walk" or "lead" while others use a tsk or clicking sound. Your dog doesn't know the meaning of the words; he will just connect the sound he hears to the task.

While out for a walk with you, your Miniature Schnauzer may slip out of his leash. This is why it is vitally important for you to train your dog to come to you on command. If he were to break free, you want to be assured that he will come back to you and not run excitedly around, ignoring your calls. Start working with your Mini Schnauzer puppy as soon as he has made himself at home. Kneel on the floor and call your pup using the command you choose, such as "come" or "here." Avoid using the dog's name because you don't want to risk the pup associating his name with being in trouble. Clap your hands to get the dog's attention and give the command. If he walks to you, reward him with ear scratches and a small treat. Repeat this exercise until your puppy is trained to come to you on command. Then you should move the exercise outside or to an unfamiliar area and continue to work on it. Soon you will be confident that he will run right back to you, when you give the command.

Training to Correct Negative Behavior

In general, Miniature Schnauzers are wonderful companion dogs, and most owners have few complaints about their behavior. However, it is your responsibility as an owner to show your Mini Schnauzer that you are the pack leader in charge and he needs to obey your orders and commands. Once the canine pecking order has been established, you should have few incidences of trouble. If the Mini Schnauzer does start to form a bad habit or two, you must immediately train your pooch to correct the negative behavior.

Stop potential chewing on important items by providing your Miniature Schnauzer puppy with lots of chew toys instead.

Miniature Schnauzer barking can occasionally be a problem, but it is one of the traits that make a Mini Schnauzer such a good guard dog. Even though barking is an innate characteristic of the breed, it is possible to train your Miniature Schnauzer to remain silent on command. First, you must figure out what is triggering your dog to bark. Once you know what the trigger is, you can try to either eliminate it or work to desensitize your dog to it. For example, many Miniature Schnauzers will bark when a stranger knocks at the door. This is because of their natural watchdog tendencies; they simply want to protect their family. You could draw the curtains so that your dog cannot see outside, or move the dog to a back room when you are expecting guests to come knocking on your door, to reduce this.

When your Mini Schnauzer starts barking, it is best to ignore him. The more you try to stop him, the more he will bark. Just ignore him and wait until he stops barking, pause a few moments, then praise his silence and reward him with a treat. Soon, your Miniature Schnauzer will realize that he will be ignored if he barks and he will be rewarded if he is silent. As a breed, the Miniature Schnauzer is very intelligent and will quickly learn to moderate their barking. They respond favorably to positive reinforcement. Conversely, they do not react well to negative reinforcement. Yelling at your barking Schnauzer or threatening to strike him will only make your dog afraid of you. It will not curb his bad behavior.

All puppies go through a bit of a chewing stage, including the Mini Schnauzer. It is the puppy's way of exploring this world and relieving the pain of teething. You can save your shoes, pillows, and table legs by teaching your puppy the command "stop" and by offering him plenty of chew toys.

Miniature Schnauzers are not an overly aggressive dog breed, but they can sometimes get feisty. If your pet shows aggression towards other dogs, children or adults, you need to nip aggressive behavior in the bud and establish yourself as the alpha in control. As soon as your Mini Schnauzer recognizes you as the dominant leader of your family pack, he will not feel the need to be the sole protector of your household. He will not react to what he perceives to be threats as aggressively as he would have.

You should never react to Miniature Schnauzer aggression with physical punishment or yelling. This will not calm your dog and will only cause more anxiety and aggression. Instead, calmly and firmly use your commands to let your pet know that his behavior is unacceptable. Also, keep in mind that dogs can sense your feelings so if you are anxious or fearful, your Mini Schnauzer may act more aggressively to protect you. Keep calm and keep your emotions in check and your dog will follow suit. Mini Schnauzer aggression towards other animals, Mini Schnauzer aggression towards children, and Mini Schnauzer aggression towards other people should not be tolerated. As a responsible dog owner, you must ensure the safety of those who come in contact with your pet.

Training for Tricks

Clever and comedic, the Miniature Schnauzer can easily master tricks that are more complex than the simple "sit," "stay," and "heel" commands. In fact, they perform well in agility and obedience. The Mini Schnauzer really wants to please his owner, and he likes to learn new things. With plenty of positive reinforcement, he can learn to stand on his hind legs and dance, or balance a dog biscuit on his snout, or catch a Frisbee.

CHAPTER 10

How Can I Keep My Miniature Schnauzer Healthy?

Your Miniature Schnauzer's job is to bring joy to your life and to be a faithful friend and companion. Your job is to make sure that your furry little best friend has the best quality of life possible. The health and safety of your Mini Schnauzer should be a priority for you. Generally speaking, Miniature Schnauzers are a healthy breed of dog with very few breed-specific genetic issues, but they still need regular veterinarian visits for checkups and troubleshooting. In fact, you should build a rapport with your veterinarian, so the two of you can form a united team to address health care concerns in your Miniature Schnauzer, as they arise. Throughout this chapter, we look at the overall health maintenance of the Miniature Schnauzer, routine medical care, and common diseases and health problems.

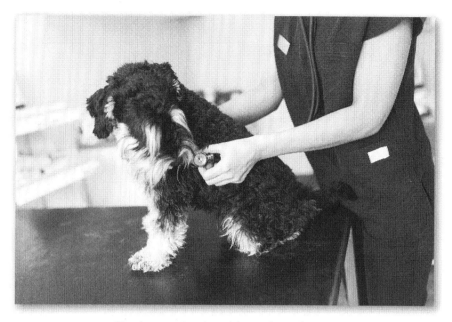

*Routine veterinarian visits are key to keeping
your Miniature Schnauzer healthy.*

Preventative Care: Miniature Schnauzer Vaccinations and Nutrition

Miniature Schnauzer health care begins with vaccinations. For the well-being of your Mini Schnauzer and the other dogs he comes into contact with, you must strictly follow the recommended vaccination routine. There is a set of required vaccinations that your dog must have but also check with your veterinarian. Some areas have additional vaccine requirements. When you pick up your Mini Schnauzer puppy from the breeder, you will receive documentation about the vaccinations your puppy has been given. Be sure to present these to your veterinarian at your first puppy visit so they can be placed on his permanent healthcare record. Vaccines have been designed to control the diseases and work best when responsible pet owners keep their dogs on a strict vaccination schedule and stay current with the shots.

Puppies are born with some antibodies from their mothers in their systems that protect them for the first eight weeks of their lives. Vaccines inject a suppressed or dead version of the disease into the dog. The disease is so weakened that it will not make the animal sick, but it will trigger an immune response in the dog's body. The dog will begin to produce antibodies to fight off this specific disease. These antibodies lay in wait, prepared to engage in combat with the disease if it ever aggressively invades or attacks the body.

At the ages of seven weeks, ten weeks, thirteen weeks and sixteen weeks, your Miniature Schnauzer puppy will need to have vaccinations for parvovirus, distemper, hepatitis, parainfluenza, and leptospirosis. These are typically combined into one injection, called a DHLP-P vaccination. In addition to the required vaccines, your Mini Schnauzer puppy may need an inoculation for internasal bordetella between the ages of eight and sixteen weeks if he was kept in a kennel with other dogs. The internasal bordetella vaccine protects the pup from a condition called kennel cough. If you intend to leave your Miniature Schnauzer at a doggie daycare or kennel, you will be required to show proof of having the internasal bordetella vaccine. You will most likely need to repeat the internasal bordetella vaccine every six months if your puppy is in regular contact with other dogs.

Puppy Age	Recommended Vaccines	Optional Vaccines
6-8 weeks	Distemper, measles, parainfluenza	Bordetella
10-12 weeks	DHPP (vaccines for distemper, adenovirus [hepatitis], parainfluenza, and parvovirus)	Coronavirus, Leptospirosis, Bordetella, Lyme disease
12-24 weeks	Rabies	None
14-16 weeks	DHPP	Coronavirus, Lyme disease, Leptospirosis
12-16 months	Rabies, DHPP	Coronavirus, Lyme disease, Leptospirosis
Every 1-2 years	DHPP	Coronavirus, Lyme disease, Leptospirosis
Every 1-3 years	Rabies (check local laws)	None

Mini Schnauzer puppies will also need rabies vaccines, which are given between four and six months of age. After that, they will need a rabies shot on a yearly basis. Depending on where you live, you might also need to get a rabies booster shot for your pup midway between the initial rabies injection and the second year one. Just ask your veterinarian if this booster is recommended for dogs living in your region.

You may want to inoculate your Miniature Schnauzer puppy for some additional diseases, too. There are vaccines available for coronavirus and Lyme disease. Coronavirus is, itself, not serious or fatal to dogs, but it becomes dangerous if there are other conditions present, such as parvo. Coronavirus causes severe diarrhea in puppies. Lyme disease, often associated with tick bites, can lead to joint pain, stiffness, arthritis, and fatigue in dogs. It is dangerous, but typically not fatal, and is treated with a dose of antibiotics. One of the biggest issues with Lyme disease is that it can flare back up periodically throughout the dog's life if the animal has not been vaccinated for it.

Miniature Schnauzer Diseases: Pancreatitis

Miniature Schnauzers are slightly more prone to developing pancreatitis than some other breeds of dogs so the owners of Mini Schnauzers should be aware of the symptoms of this potentially serious disease. Miniature Schnauzer pancreatitis is, technically speaking, an inflammation of the pancreas, but it is more complex than it sounds. The role of the pancreas is to produce and release enzymes that help aid digestion. The enzymes are supposed to activate once they hit the small intestine, but sometimes they become active immediately, causing inflammation in the pancreas and the surrounding tissue. It is not only very painful for your dog, but it can lead to permanent damage to the organ.

Pancreatitis symptoms are easy to spot, but they can mimic other conditions. If your Miniature Schnauzer is exhibiting several of the following symptoms, take him to the veterinarian as soon as possible. Pancreatitis can progress quickly, so it is not a condition in which you can take a wait-and-see approach. The most common symptoms of pancreatitis include repeated vomiting, diarrhea, pain or distended abdomen, fever, weakness and fatigue, loss of appetite, and dehydration.

One of the main causes of pancreatitis is too much fat in the diet. Often it comes on after the Miniature Schnauzer eats a large quantity of fatty food at one time. For example, veterinarians often see a spike in pancreatitis cases in dogs right after the holidays because their owners had decided to treat them with a special Christmas meal of human food or holiday guests slip the dog a few bits of people food under the table. In the United States, the day after Thanksgiving is known as the day that veterinarians see the most cases of pancreatitis in dogs. The digestive systems of the Mini Schnauzers are not equipped to handle a glut of fat. Pancreatitis, however, can be caused by other factors, such as obesity, diabetes, hypothyroidism, or blunt trauma to the abdomen.

Miniature Schnauzer Diseases: Hemorrhagic Gastroenteritis

Small and miniature breeds of dogs, including the Miniature Schnauzer, are more prone to contracting hemorrhagic gastroenteritis than larger breeds of dogs. A potentially serious condition, hemorrhagic gastroenteritis presents as the sudden onset of bloody diarrhea, which can then lead to dehydration and shock. The cause of hemorrhagic gastroenteritis is unknown, but the Schnauzer should be treated immediately to relieve diarrhea and dehydration, which can be life-threatening. In fact, the way hemorrhagic gastroenteritis is treated is by addressing the symptoms…reducing or stopping diarrhea and treating the dehydration with fluids.

Miniature Schnauzer Diseases: Epilepsy

Miniature Schnauzer epilepsy is not uncommon and may be caused by an inherited condition. These are known as idiopathic or primary seizures. Your dog may also have secondary or reactive seizures. A secondary seizure is related to trauma or injury, stroke, or brain tumors. A reactive seizure could result from the brain reacting to a toxin, low blood sugar, or another sort of metabolic problem. The onset of seizures in Miniature Schnauzers happens between six months and three years old. If your Mini Schnauzer has a seizure, your veterinarian may do blood work to rule out accidental poisoning. Your dog will be put on an anti-seizure medication that he will need to take diligently for the rest of his life. Routine blood testing will be able to help your veterinarian gauge the effectiveness of the medication and adjust the dosing if needed.

If your Mini Schnauzer has a seizure, you should do what you can to keep him from injuring himself. This includes removing nearby items that he may knock over or moving him to a safe place, like the floor if he was sitting on the couch. Don't try to hold his mouth open or control his tongue, as you might do with a human having a seizure. The dog is not in control of his actions during a seizure and may bite at you. Also, do not try to hold him still or stop his limbs from moving. You may inadvertently injure him. You can calmly stroke his head or back and speak in a slow, quiet, and reassuring voice to him. When he comes out of the seizure, continue to comfort him and try to keep him calm. He may lose control of his bowels or bladder so be ready with a puppy pad or some newspaper. Once you are sure the seizure is over, offer him a drink or water. The seizure is hard on your little Miniature Schnauzer's body…akin to running a marathon…so he will be tired and thirsty.

Take note of the seizure and anything that may have triggered it, the duration, etc. Share this information with your veterinarian, so the two of you can determine a course of action.

Miniature Schnauzer Diseases: Diabetes

Just like in humans, Miniature Schnauzer diabetes results from the dog's body's inability to regulate the blood sugar levels because the insulin level is deficient. Insulin is responsible for the body's ability to break down and store glucose, a simple sugar that provides the animal with the energy it needs to function. If the insulin production slows, the glucose stays in the bloodstream of the Mini Schnauzer and doesn't progress to the body cells. The cells then send messages to the dog's liver to produce a glucose-like substance, called glycogen. The liver releases glycogen into the already-flooded bloodstream, spiking the glucose levels even higher. Left untreated, Miniature Schnauzer diabetes can lead to coma, blindness, and even death.

Mini Schnauzer owners need to keep an eye out for signs and symptoms of diabetes in their dogs, but it is often difficult. The symptoms are typically minor or subtle at first and get progressively worse. Look for excessive thirst in your dog, along with sudden weight gain or loss, frequent urination or accidents in the house, a sudden increase or decrease in appetite, and vision changes. Schedule a veterinarian visit, if you suspect that your Miniature Schnauzer may have diabetes. A simple blood test will confirm this. Then, you can work with your veterinarian to establish a treatment plan that will help your Mini Schnauzer regain his health and avoid the complications that can come from uncontrolled blood sugar levels.

Miniature Schnauzer diabetes is manageable with lifestyle changes. After a diabetes diagnosis, your veterinarian will probably change your Miniature Schnauzer's diet to one that is low in fat and carbohydrates, but high in fiber. You may have to give your pet insulin injections. You will also need to make sure that your dog gets regular exercise as well.

Miniature Schnauzer Allergies and Skin Problems

It is estimated that roughly one-quarter of all dogs suffer from some sort of allergy. If your Miniature Schnauzer is one of them, he may constantly scratch at his skin or ears, rub his face, lick his paws, or shake. All of these are signs that your Mini Schnauzer may be having a reaction to an allergen.

Miniature Schnauzers, along with all other dog breeds, can encounter five different types of allergies: food allergies, inhalant allergies, contact allergies, bacterial allergies, and flea allergies. While many of the symptoms, such as scratching, chewing and licking, are the same for all types of allergies, some may include more serious reactions, like vomiting and diarrhea.

Some dogs are sensitive to food items, including eggs, fish, milk, corn, wheat, and more. If you suspect that your Miniature Schnauzer is experiencing allergies related to his food, your veterinarian may put him on an anti-allergy diet for a month or two. The anti-allergy diet will probably consist of oatmeal, pumpkin, venison, rice, and sweet potatoes. If the allergy symptoms subside after eating the anti-allergy diet, different foods are then slowly introduced back into the dog's diet. This way, you should be able to learn what the trigger food is so you can avoid giving it to your dog in the future.

Inhalant allergies are the most common type of dog allergies. Pollen, mold, dust mites, and cigarette smoke can all cause inhalant allergies in Miniature Schnauzers. Your dog will react to these triggers by scratching or coughing. Fortunately, your veterinarian will be able to do an intradermal skin test to find the trigger that is causing the allergic reactions. You should then attempt to remove the trigger and also give the dog more frequent baths to remove the inhalants from his fur. If you cannot remove the offending trigger, your veterinarian may prescribe allergy shots, steroids, or antihistamines.

Contact allergies are the least common type of canine allergies. Caused by direct contact with an irritant such as a flea collar, bedding material, or carpet, these allergies manifest as itching, redness, and swelling. To determine the offending irritant, your veterinarian may do a skin scrape test. Since the results of this test may not point to a specific item, you may have to do some detective work to find the allergen. Once you do, the treatment for contact allergies is as simple as removing the irritant.

For Miniature Schnauzers with suppressed or weakened immune systems, the Staphylococcus bacteria on the dog's skin may cause an allergy and skin problems. You may see your dog scratching, or you may observe patches of hair loss and an odor coming from his skin. A blood test will show if your Miniature Schnauzer is suffering from a bacterial allergy. A positive result will mean that your veterinarian will prescribe an antibiotic.

Flea saliva and bites are common allergens for Miniature Schnauzers and other dogs. Flea bites are always a bit annoying for dogs, but if you see your dog excessively scratching and chewing on his skin, he could be experiencing an allergic reaction. It can be so itchy that the dog will scratch until he has open sores and hair loss. The sores may become infected. The first step in alleviating flea allergies is, of course, to control fleas. Take aggressive steps to remove fleas from your dog and from your home. Just one flea can quickly cause an infestation if you aren't careful. Every day, you should spread flea powder on the carpeted areas of your home and vacuum. This will help keep fleas at bay. But you should also routinely groom and bathe your Miniature Schnauzer, too.

Miniature Schnauzer Eye Disorders

Mini Schnauzer eyes can be the source of disease or disorders. From cataracts to glaucoma and more, it is important for pet owners to know the warning signs of eye problems in Miniature Schnauzers.

Cataracts are cloudiness in the lens of the dog's eyes. The cloudiness can be minor or completely opaque, causing vision loss. Cataracts are inherited and common in many breeds of dogs, including Miniature Schnauzers. Risk factors for cataracts include diabetes, advanced age, and low calcium levels. Depending on the severity and speed of progression of cataracts, your veterinarian may suggest surgery.

Glaucoma is marked by pressure in the eye which can lead to optic nerve damage and maybe even blindness. In nearly half of all cases of glaucoma in Miniature Schnauzers, blindness occurs within a year, despite surgical or medical intervention. Among the symptoms of glaucoma in Mini Schnauzers are excessive blinking, dilated pupils, high pressure in the eyeball, blood vessels in the whites of the eyes, and vision loss.

Some breeds of dog, including Mini Schnauzers, may get progressive retinal atrophy, a condition in which there is a degeneration of the retinal tissue. For Mini Schnauzers, the disease will present between three and six years of age. The onset of the disease is slow and gradual, and it is easy to miss the early signs. The vision slowly dims over time. There is no cure for progressive retinal atrophy, but it is important to identify breeding dogs affected by it, to stop the spread of the condition.

CHAPTER 11

What Do I Need to Know about Miniature Schnauzer Tail Docking and Ear Cropping?

At some point in time, humans decided to surgically alter the appearance of the Miniature Schnauzer, especially purebred Mini Schnauzers used for show, by docking their tails and cropping their ears. Although this considered the accepted practice for decades, it is not without its controversies. Today, the debate rages over ethical concerns about tail docking and ear cropping in all dog breeds, including the Mini Schnauzer. In this chapter, we will take a closer look at the practice of tail docking and ear cropping as they apply to the Miniature Schnauzer and examine the legal and ethical issues of this common practice.

*Ear cropping is a cosmetic procedure done
to alter the appearance of the dog.*

What is Miniature Schnauzer Tail Docking?

Tail docking is the surgical removal of a dog's tail, often without anesthesia, when the animal is a young puppy. Although it has been a common procedure for many years, attitudes are now changing. Tail docking is now illegal in the United Kingdom and generally frowned upon, if not outright banned, in most European countries. It remains commonplace across the United States and Canada, and neither country has a national law banning the practice. Instead, it is up to the individual state or province to pass legislation addressing the issue of tail docking. Several Canadian provinces have outlawed the procedure, as have a few U.S. states.

Under pressure from animal activist groups, most national dog associations worldwide have placed restrictions on tail docking or banned it outright. It is now not uncommon to see purebred Miniature Schnauzers with docked tails competing in the show ring with dogs with their natural tails, at dog shows in England and throughout Europe. In the United States, however, the American Kennel Club still maintains that docked tails as their breed standard for the Mini Schnauzer, although many veterinarian organizations oppose tail docking for cosmetic reasons. The AKC maintains, however, that tail docking in the Miniature Schnauzer is not an unnecessary cosmetic procedure, but one that is done to promote the welfare of the breed and the health of the individual dog.

Miniature Schnauzer tail docking began in the early days of the breed, more than one hundred and fifty years ago. One of the original reasons for removing the dogs' tails was to reduce the chances of the animal contracting rabies, but we know today that the tail of a dog has nothing to do with rabies as a disease. Another early reason for tail docking was to reduce the risk of injury or bites to the tail when the Miniature Schnauzer was rooting out mice and rats on the farm. It was also believed in the 1800s that a dog's back would be stronger and straighter if his tail was removed. For these reasons, tail docking was included in the breed standards for Mini Schnauzers when the dog breed was first recognized and registered.

But the Miniature Schnauzer didn't remain a working dog on the farm. His sunny disposition and guard dog tendencies led this breed to become a house dog, a companion dog rather than a working dog. Yet the docked tail remained a feature of the breed.

As a historical side note, tail docking was done for tax purposes in 17th and 18th century England. Working dogs were not taxed, but companion dogs were. Farmers docked the tails of their herding, hunting, and ratting dogs as a way to signify to the tax collectors that these are working animals, and therefore, untaxable. For the wealthy upper class, hunting with dogs was a leisurely pastime. They would intentionally leave their hunting dogs unaltered as a way to flaunt their wealth and demonstrate to the community that they could afford to pay the tail tax on their dogs. This dog tail tax was repealed in the closing years of the 1700s, but by then it was so ingrained in the culture of the country that most working dogs continued to have their tails docked.

In the past, tail docking of Miniature Schnauzers and other dog breeds was a procedure that was done at home by untrained dog breeders. Obviously, this increased the odds of infection or botched docking. It was also typically done without pain medicine for the animal, causing them undue stress, discomfort, and leading to trauma and distrust of humans. Today, if the dog breeder chooses to dock the tails of their Mini Schnauzer puppies, they hire a licensed veterinarian to do the procedure in a sterile environment. Most often, it is done when the puppies are very young – only three to five days old – to minimize the risk of infection or reinjuring the wound. For reputable breeders, the health and well-being of the Miniature Schnauzer puppy is paramount, and they will take every precaution to protect their investment so they can offer a happy and healthy puppy for potential buyers.

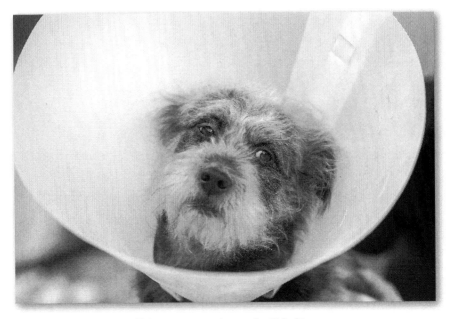

*Discuss ear cropping and tail docking
with your breeder and veterinarian.*

What is Miniature Schnauzer Ear Cropping?

Even more controversial than tail docking is ear cropping in
Mini Schnauzers. With ear cropping, part of the dog's natural
ear is removed so that the ear will stand erect, giving the animal
an alert and polished appearance. Although supporters of the
practice claim that ear cropping reduces chronic ear infections in
dogs, there has been no evidence that this is the case. Rather, it
seems, ear cropping in Miniature Schnauzers is done strictly for
cosmetic purposes.

Miniature Schnauzer ear cropping originally started as a way
to protect the dog from snagging his ears when hunting mice
and rats. The shorter ears, it was claimed, also improved the air
flow into the ear canal, reducing ear odor and infections. But the

inclusion of ear cropping as part of the Mini Schnauzer breed standard meant that the practice stuck around long after the dog breed transitioned from a working dog to a companion dog.

Today, ear cropping is seen as a form of animal cruelty, and many countries and national canine clubs have lifted the breed standards pertaining to ear cropping. The practice is banned in the United Kingdom. The American Kennel Club, however, no longer requires ear docking for registered Mini Schnauzers, but has not yet banned the procedure outright.

If a dog owner chooses to have their Mini Schnauzer puppy's ears cropped, they should only have it done by a licensed veterinarian who can perform the surgery with the minimal amount of pain and distress on the animal and a reduced chance for infection. A veterinarian will only do the surgery on puppies that are at least seven or eight weeks old. If you visit a Miniature Schnauzer breeder who has puppies under the age of eight weeks with cropped ears, you should question who did the procedure and where. Although the practice is falling out of fashion, some Mini Schnauzer breeders may still crop the puppies' ears at home, most likely without anesthesia or antiseptic conditions. Naturally, this is traumatic and dangerous for the poor puppies. If every person interested in purchasing a Mini Schnauzer puppy walked away from breeders who performed home ear cropping, these breeders would eventually learn that saving the cost of vet bills at the expense of the puppies will not pay off in the end. Future Miniature Schnauzer owners want a dog that has been well-cared for its entire life and is as happy and trusting as it is healthy.

CHAPTER 12

Should I Show My Miniature Schnauzer in Dog Shows?

Participating in dog shows is a fun pastime and a great way to connect with other Miniature Schnauzer enthusiasts. It is also a way to hold your Mini Schnauzer up against others in the spirit of competition. The basic goal of a dog show is to evaluate breeding stock so the dogs, in a sense, are not being compared to each other as much as they are being compared against the published breed standards of the Miniature Schnauzer breed. So what do you need to know before you decide if showing your Miniature Schnauzer in dog shows is what you want to do?

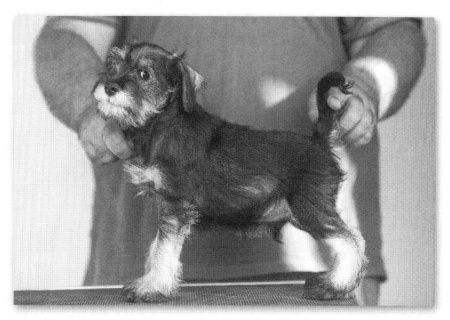

Setting the dog up in a standard position will allow the judges to compare each Miniature Schnauzer dog against the breed standards.

Showing Breeding Stock

Dog breed clubs and national dog organizations host dog shows in many countries. Each club and organization maintains a set of breed standards by which the dog is judged. The Miniature Schnauzer is no exception. One important thing to keep in mind is that dogs shown in the conformation classes at dog shows must be unaltered, meaning they cannot be spayed or neutered. This is because the dog is being evaluated as a breeding stock animal – in essence, a dog with the ability to produce a superior litter of puppies. If you are considering showing your Miniature Schnauzer, you must decide not to spay or neuter your puppy.

Your first step to entering the world of dog showing is to acquire a high-quality Miniature Schnauzer puppy from a reputable breeder who has bred their puppies to the national standards. The step after that is to join a local Miniature Schnauzer club. Your Miniature Schnauzer club will most likely be an invaluable source of information about the Mini Schnauzer breed, and about dog showing in general. The club will also have information about upcoming shows.

In addition to showing for breed standards,
Miniature Schnauzers can be used for agility shows.

Understanding Dog Breed Groups

When showing Miniature Schnauzers, it is important to understand the breed group to which the Mini Schnauzer belongs. It is not as cut and dry as it is with other dog breeds. The American Kennel Club has eight groups – the hound group, the terrier group, the toy group, the sporting group, the non-sporting group, the working group, the herding group, and the miscellaneous group. The Miniature Schnauzer is shown in the terrier group, while the Standard Schnauzer and the Giant Schnauzer are both shown in the working class. The Miniature Schnauzer is also shown in the terrier group as part of the Canadian Kennel Club organization. The Kennel Club of the UK classifies dogs into seven groups – the terrier group, the hound group, the working group, the pastoral group, the utility group, the gundog group, and the toy group. With the UK Kennel Club, the Miniature Schnauzer is found in the utility group. In the New Zealand Kennel Club, the Miniature Schnauzer is a member of the working group.

The American Kennel Club and the Canadian Kennel Club recognize three coat colors for Miniature Schnauzers. Those are black, salt and pepper, and black and silver. Only dogs with one of these coats are recognized by these two clubs. However, white Miniature Schnauzers are recognized in other countries and by the Federation Cynologique Internationale, the largest international federation of kennel clubs. White Mini Schnauzers can be shown in most European countries. The controversy stems from questions and debates about the white variant gene and where it originates from. Is the gene present in the originally recognized breed or did it develop later, as a result of breeding modifications? Because the original German breed standards for the Miniature Schnauzer did not list white as an accepted coat color, American and Canadian kennel clubs will not recognize it.

If you decide to show your Miniature Schnauzer, you must work with your animal and train him for the show ring. You must also commit to grooming him to meet acceptable standards and feeding him for optimal health and body stature. Dog showing is not an inexpensive hobby and cutting corners will not win ribbons. It can be a pleasurable and rewarding pursuit for you and your dog if you choose to put in the effort and expense.

CHAPTER 13

What Do I Need to Know About Miniature Schnauzer Grooming?

Miniature Schnauzers are handsome little dogs. It takes a little bit of work to keep them looking their best. Mini Schnauzer grooming can be done at home, or you can take your dog to a professional groomer who has been trained to care for Schnauzers. The Miniature Schnauzer coat is a bit tricky, as it is a double-coat. The topcoat is wiry and stiff, and the undercoat is soft and fluffier. You need to be able to groom both parts of the dog's coat in order for the Mini Schnauzer to look his very best.

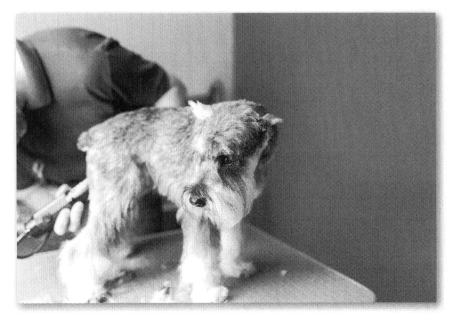

Regular grooming will keep your
Miniature Schnauzer looking handsome.

Miniature Schnauzer Grooming Tools

Before you can groom your Miniature Schnauzer, you need to have the proper tools on hand. These include brushes, clippers, scissors, and nail clippers. The right Mini Schnauzer grooming equipment will mean a less stressful grooming experience for your dog.

For the Mini Schnauzer's double coat, a slicker brush works quite well. Slicker brushes have a cluster of short, metal tines or pins that are slightly bent at the ends. The slicker brush is designed to reach through the wiry outer coat to get to the finer inner coat. It is also ideal for smoothing out tangles or matted hair. Look for slicker brushes with blunted ends as these are more comfortable for the dog.

Electric clippers will help you trim your Mini Schnauzer and give his coat a sleek and polished appearance. You can find corded clippers, as well as a cordless one that allows you more freedom when grooming your pet. Ideally, you should select a clipper with detachable blades. The blades will be numbered, and the higher numbered blades will give you a closer cut. For Miniature Schnauzer grooming, you will use a #10 blade on the overall body and a #30 or #40 blade on the ears.

A nice pair of sharpened scissors will allow you to put the finishing touches on your Miniature Schnauzer. Scissors will help you get a clean line on the dog's coat. You can find dog grooming scissors in every price point, from the cheap to the ultra-expensive. You should look for good quality scissors that are durable, sharp, and straight, but the most costly pair of scissors is not necessary. A decent, mid-range pair will be sufficient.

Miniature Schnauzer Toenail Grooming

Depending on the rate of growth and how much your dog wears down his toenails naturally, you may need to trim your Mini Schnauzer's nails weekly or bi-weekly. Investing in a decent pair of nail clippers will make this task easier for both you and your pet. You will find two different types of doggie nail clippers on the market. One is a scissor-like clipper, and the other is a guillotine style. Both types of clippers will get the job done and choosing between the two is a matter of personal preference. You should also have some styptic powder on hand to help stop the bleeding if you happen to clip the nail down a little too much.

Miniature Schnauzer Bathing

Before you bathe or clip your Miniature Schnauzer, thoroughly brush him and remove all knots or clumps of fur. Unfortunately, you may find that the most mats and knots are in the beard, belly, underarms, and legs of your dog. These are the most tender areas for you to brush, so be gentle as you work through the snarls. In fact, you should brush these regions frequently to minimize matting.

You can bathe your Miniature Schnauzer often. Most Mini Schnauzer owners wash their dogs once a week, and others do it once a month…and all times in between. No matter how often you bathe your pooch, you should wash his beard more often. The Miniature Schnauzer beard gets wet and dirty very easily. It is dragged through his food bowl and water bowl and along the ground and is the receptacle for his slobber. To wash just his beard, you can use a spray bottle or small tub, or lift your dog into the sink. The tub or sink will also work for a full bath. Make sure the water is not too hot and not too cold. A good quality dog shampoo will loosen the dirt in his fur and leave him clean and smelling great. Around the face and beard, you should use a tearless shampoo and avoid getting it in his eyes. Be sure you thoroughly rinse his fur to remove any suds. If shampoo is left in his fur, it attracts dirt and can become matted.

Miniature Schnauzer Blow Drying

After his bath, dry your Mini Schnauzer with a towel. You can blow dry his fur using a blow dryer on medium heat and a brush. As you blow dry, brush the dog's beard and eyebrows forwards and downward. For the legs, start at the top and work your way down, brushing the hair up. Make sure the fur is completely dry, otherwise the leg hair will lose its fluffiness and look limp.

Regular grooming will keep the Mini Schnauzer's fur tangle-free.

Miniature Schnauzer Grooming and Clipping

It is possible, with a bit of practice, to clip your Miniature Schnauzer yourself. You can save the cost of regular groomer visits by following the recommended Schnauzer clipping procedure. You can watch YouTube videos on Miniature Schnauzer clipping to help you see how the process works.

For the body of the Mini Schnauzer, you will most likely use the #10 blade on your clipper. Keep the clipper against the dog's skin, holding the skin tight, and smoothly clip the fur. Start at the base of the dog's head and go down the neck and back and along the sides of the animal. Clip the throat, cheeks, and head against the grain. Clip the sides to blend evenly into the underbelly, creating a defined line. Take extreme caution when clipping the dog's belly and genital area. Stop the body clip at the elbow and the bend of the hind leg. Every so often, feel the blade of the clippers to make sure they are not getting overheated. If they feel too warm, spray the blade with clipper spray to cool it down.

Switch to a #30 or #40 blade and clip the Mini Schnauzer's ears and the pads of its paws, also going against the grain. Use scissors to trim up the front legs. First, comb the leg hair straight out from the leg. Then, pointing your scissors downward, trim the fur in a circular manner while combing it outward, until you achieve the desired length. Trip the hair on the hind legs to follow the curve of the leg. Trim the underbelly fur so that it tapers towards the hind legs.

You can carefully use the scissors to trim up the hairs growing inside your dog's ears and between the pads of his paws. Be as careful as you can be and keep your dog still during this process. The scissors also come in handy for evening out the Mini Schnauzer's eyebrows and beard. Comb the beard forward and trim it to align with the widest part of his skull.

Miniature Schnauzer Dental Care

As part of his regular grooming routine, you should brush your Miniature Schnauzer's teeth. This will help control breath odor and will remove tartar that can build up on his teeth. You can purchase a doggie toothbrush and toothpaste at a pet supply store.

Miniature Schnauzer Anal Gland Care

The final part of the Miniature Schnauzer grooming ritual is, perhaps, the most unpleasant. It is anal gland care. Fortunately, Miniature Schnauzers are not prone to anal gland clogging like some other dog breeds are, however, if your dog scoots along the floor or licks his anus or has a pungent odor coming from his backside, he may be experiencing an anal gland problem.

The anal glands are the dog's natural scent glands. They are located on either side of the anus at the 4 o'clock and 8 o'clock positions. The gland produces a watery, brown liquid that serves as a lubricant for bowel movements. Each dog produces a unique scent from its anal glands, and this becomes the dog's calling card. This is why dogs will sniff each other's rear ends when they meet.

Bath time is the ideal time to manually express your Miniature Schnauzer's anal glands if you think it is necessary to do so. Before you attempt it on your own, discuss it with your veterinarian. You certainly don't want to cause harm or injury to your pet. To start, stand your dog up and place a warm, wet washcloth on the anus opening to relax the area. Then cover the anus opening with a disposable wet wipe and locate the anal glands. Place your index finger on one gland and your thumb on the other and firmly press inward and upward toward the anus, moving your fingers together until they meet. This will force the expression of the anal gland fluids and unclog any blockage. A word of warning, however; the fluid has a foul stench to it and will squirt out suddenly. Don't get too close. Be sure to clean the area thoroughly when you are done. The chances are good that you will not have to do this with your Miniature Schnauzer and if you are skittish about it, schedule a vet visit and leave the professionals to do this task.

CHAPTER 14

What Do I Need to Know About Miniature Schnauzer Breeding, Pregnancy, and Birth?

A fter your first Miniature Schnauzer, you will probably fall in love with the whole breed. If you decide to try your hand at breeding your Mini Schnauzer, you need to make sure that you are doing so safely and responsibly, with the best interest of the dog and the breed in mind. You need to understand the best practices for selecting a mate and preparing your Mini Schnauzer to be bred. You also need to understand the Miniature Schnauzer heat cycle and know how to care for a pregnant Mini Schnauzer. We will also examine labor, delivery, and newborn puppy care.

The average little size of a Miniature Schnauzer is three to eight pups.

How to Find A Mate for Your Miniature Schnauzer

The first step in breeding your Miniature Schnauzer is to select the breeding parents. You can breed your own Schnauzers if they were born to different parents, or you can seek out a male, or sire, or a female, or bitch, for breeding purposes. Finding a Miniature Schnauzer mate can be a daunting task, but one you should take seriously. Don't settle for the first mate you find. It is more important to be selective. Talk to trusted and reputable Miniature Schnauzer breeders in your area and to local veterinarians and let them know what you are looking for in a mate. Seek out dogs that are registered, have a favorable personality and even temperament, and are generally in good health.

What is the Miniature Schnauzer Heat Cycle?

Once you have selected a mate, you must be sure that the female Miniature Schnauzer is fertile, following her heat cycle. The female Mini Schnauzer will go into heat twice a year, and her heat cycle will last for about 21 days. Her fertile period comes approximately 10 to 14 days into her heat cycle after her discharge becomes clear. While she is in heat, be sure to keep your Miniature Schnauzer female away from all male dogs. The scent given off by a female Mini Schnauzer in heat attracts male dogs of all breeds. She can be impregnated by a random dog, which would destroy the purity of her puppies. Interestingly, puppies in a single litter can have different fathers, if the mother mated with multiple dogs. For this reason, it is vital that she is protected from aggressive male dogs who want to mate with her. Keep her locked in a secure kennel during her heat cycle.

Before you put the male and female dogs together, check the female for signs that she is fertile. You don't want to put the male with the female until you know she is ready to mate. The male Miniature Schnauzer, no matter how docile he may normally be, may be so aroused by the female's scent that he acts out aggressively toward her. To determine the fertility of the female, you can ask your veterinarian to check her hormone levels. Or you can see if she "flags." Try scratching her skin at the base of her tail. If she is ready to mate, she will involuntarily lift her tail and wag it side to side as if it were a flag, beckoning mates to her.

Miniature Schnauzer Mating

Actually mating the two dogs is quite simple. Just put the two animals together and let nature take its course. Introduce the male into the female's kennel and keep an eye out for mating activity. The female Miniature Schnauzer can become pregnant after one mating, but you will want to make sure it took. Put the male and female together, perhaps every other day, and allow them to mate repeatedly. When her fertile period has come to an end, the female Mini Schnauzer will refuse to mate. Her rebuke is her signal that you can stop arranging the mating activities.

It will take about one month before you know if the Miniature Schnauzer is, indeed, pregnant. Signs of pregnancy in your Mini Schnauzer include weight gain and protruding nipples. These same symptoms could, however, indicate a false pregnancy. Your veterinarian will be able to do a doggie ultrasound to confirm her pregnancy.

Miniature Schnauzer Pregnancy

Miniature Schnauzers have a gestational period of approximately 63 days. During this time, be sure the mother-to-be is well-cared for. Creating new life can be taxing for your Mini Schnauzer mama, and you will want to keep her happy, healthy, and thriving during this time. Discuss her changing nutritional needs with your veterinarian and adjust her diet as necessary. Monitor her exercise levels and take care that she doesn't over-exert herself.

How Do I Prepare for My Miniature Schnauzer to Give Birth?

As your Miniature Schnauzer mother-to-be approaches her due date, you will need to have a birthing area prepared for her. It could be a box lined with soft blankets or towels or a crate, also lined with soft material, or a doggie bed in a quiet corner. Allow her to become familiar with the space and become comfortable there. Ideally, she will go there when labor starts. Despite your advanced planning, she may decide to have her puppies somewhere else, like in a closet or on your bed. Early in the labor stage, you can gently encourage her to move to the birthing box. However, keep in mind that there may have been a reason she rejected it in the first place. Perhaps it was in a spot that was too noisy or busy.

If you want to be sure you know when labor is starting, begin taking your Mini Schnauzer's temperature a few weeks prior to her due date. Her body temperature will probably be a normal 105.5 degrees Fahrenheit, but as labor starts, her temperature will drop. She will also appear a little bit anxious or jumpy, lick herself more, or seek a secluded area. Let her go. As tempting as it is to follow her around during this time, allow her some privacy. At minimal allow her privacy until active delivery begins.

Miniature Schnauzer Labor and Delivery

In most cases, your Mini Schnauzer mama does not need your help during labor and delivery. It is, after all, a very natural process. When active labor starts, the Miniature Schnauzer mother may shiver or pant. Don't be concerned; this is normal. You may notice the contractions of her uterus when you look at her flanks, and you may observe a clear discharge leaking from her. As her contractions get stronger, the first puppy is born. Resist the urge to cheer excitedly! Instead, keep your voice low and calm as you praise the Miniature Schnauzer mother.

In general, the puppies will arrive within twenty minutes of each other. It is an exhausting endeavor, however, and the mama may take a break halfway through to rest. It is not uncommon for her to rest for a couple hours before she pushes out the rest of her puppies. The entire process can last from three to twelve hours. The average litter size of the Miniature Schnauzer is between three to eight puppies.

When a puppy arrives, the mother will bite through the sac and the umbilical cord, and then will lick the puppy clean. If another puppy's arrival interrupts the process, don't feel as though you need to help. The Miniature Schnauzer mother will get back to the task at hand as soon as she can. Don't panic if you see some of the puppies making their appearances tail first. That is not uncommon. If the puppy seems stuck in the birth canal, you can gently assist, taking care not to tug.

Puppies need to be socialized from an early age.

Newborn Miniature Schnauzer Puppy Care

Once you are certain that your Mini Schnauzer mother has delivered all her puppies, and you know that all is well, offer her some food and water. She may also need to go outside to relieve her bladder, but she won't leave her puppies if she feels they may be in danger. You and the rest of the family should leave the area and give the mother some alone time with her babies and a chance to see that it is safe to leave them for a few moments. When you are able, remove the soiled bedding and replace it with clean, dry bedding.

The puppies will be small and helpless for the first few weeks, spending the majority of their time nursing, sleeping, and bonding with their mother and litter mates. Soon, however, they will play and run and melt your heart with their cuteness.

Of course, you cannot keep all of the puppies, as much as you may want to. Ideally, you've found good homes for most of them before they were even born, but if not, you need to work on securing them, good homes. You can ask at your veterinarian's office or a local Miniature Schnauzer club to see if you can get the word out about your Mini Schnauzer puppies. Keep in mind that you will need to take all the puppies in for their first veterinarian visit and the first round of vaccines before they leave to live with their new families.

CHAPTER 15

What are Common Miniature Schnauzer Mixes?

The size and temperament of the Miniature Schnauzer makes it a popular dog for mixed breeding. Controlled mixed breeding by reputable dog breeders creates what are called designer dogs. Designer dogs have enjoyed a spike in popularity in recent years. It is important to understand that mixed breeding does not create a whole new dog breed. Rather, what is produced is a cross between two established dog breeds. One advantage of owning a mixed breed dog is that they often have fewer health issues because their gene pool is more diverse. Another benefit is that the puppies will have traits or characteristics that differ from the ones common to one breed.

Although mixed breed dogs are not eligible to participate in purebred dog shows, designer dog breeders have created a wide array of adorable Miniature Schnauzer mixes that are really wonderful companion and family dogs. We will take a brief look at some of the common Mini Schnauzer mixes – with their clever blended names – and the benefits of these designer mixed breeds, within this chapter.

The Schnoodle is a mix between a Miniature Schnauzer and a Poodle.

Chizer

The Chizer is a mix between a Miniature Schnauzer and a Chihuahua that was officially recognized in the U.S. Designer Canine Registry in 2009. Bred as a companion dog, the Chizer is tiny – less than 15 pounds – with characteristic large ears. The Chizer has a short neck and bright, round eyes. The Chizer has a short coat, but it may be in an array of colors from white and gray, to brown and black. If the Chizer has inherited specific traits from its Chihuahua parent, he may not be ideally suited for households with small children.

Schapso

The 10 to 15 pound (4.53 to 6.80 kilograms) Schapso is a fun-sized, lovable mix of a Miniature Schnauzer and a Lhasa Apso. Generally a healthy and long-lived dog, the Schapso is well-suited for apartments or small houses. A characteristic of the Schapso is that he is a cuddler who tends to stick close to his owner. Loyal and comical, the Schapso has floppy ears, and a thick, straight coat and the majority of this designer breed has Schnauzer-like beards.

Snorkie

A popular designer hybrid, the Snorkie is produced by breeding a Miniature Schnauzer with a Yorkshire Terrier. This sweet and lovable little dog rarely gets bigger than eleven pounds. Snorkies are energetic and athletic, with a pleasant disposition that makes him a good family dog. Snorkies tend to look more like their Yorkshire Terrier parent with straight and silky fur. Many Snorkies, however, get their gray coloring from their Miniature Schnauzer parent. The silky fur of the Snorkie requires some maintenance and upkeep to prevent tangling. In fact, many Snorkie owners opt for a short haircut as a way to solve this issue.

Pom-A-Nauze

Both the Miniature Schnauzer and the Pomeranian are dog breeds that originated in Germany as ratting dogs, so it was only natural that designer dog breeders put these two breeds together to produce the Pom-A-Nauze. The small Pom-A-Nauze can adopt the appearance and traits of either of its parents, but you should find all Pom-A-Nauzes to be friendly, intelligent, playful, and independent. A drawback of the Pom-A-Nauze is that it inherits a barking tendency from both parents, so owners of this designer breed should be consistently prepared to train their dog to refrain from barking excessively.

Schnoxie

Created by breeding Miniature Schnauzers with Daschunds, the personable Schnoxie is a small, but muscular hybrid with either smooth, straight coats or thick, wiry ones. A benefit of the Schnoxie is that they do not shed very much and are considered hypoallergenic. Smart and trainable, the Schnoxie can be rather vocal and protective, but loyal and charismatic.

Schnug

The Schnug, a mix of the Miniature Schnauzer and the Pug, is a small designer dog with a long body and short tail. The Schnug is often described as boxy, short-legged pooch. Lively and smart, the friendly Schnug is full of life, but they can also be feisty and stubborn at times. The Schnug adores attention and can easily be talked into snuggling on your lap. His intelligent and pleasing nature means that he is easily trained, but he may choose to ignore your command in an attempt to show that he is the boss. You will need to establish yourself as the leader of the pack.

Mauzer

The cross between a Miniature Schnauzer and a Maltese, called a Mauzer, is a small dog that rarely tops twenty pounds (9.07 kilograms). No one has told the Mauzer that he is small, however. He is a great watchdog who will not hesitate to alert his owners to anything he thinks may be a threat. The Mauzer is ideally suited as a companion for singles or seniors, not for families with young children. Depending on which of his parents has the more dominant genes, the Mauzer could look more like a Miniature Schnauzer, or more like a Maltese.

Schnekingese

When a Miniature Schnauzer is bred with a Pekingese, the result is a sturdy and energetic little dog known as the Schenkingese. Depending on which parent had the dominant genes, the Schnekingese can have wiry fur with a thick undercoat or longer, softer fur. The Schnekingese tend to have adorable floppy ears and black, brown, tan, or white fur. Described as active and affectionate, the Schnekingese can sometimes be easily distracted and therefore, may not be a good watchdog, despite his barking tendencies. The Schnekingese mix has a high prey drive instinct and may not tolerate other animals in his household.

Schnocker

Cuddly and cute, the Schnocker is a designer hybrid of the Miniature Schnauzer and the Cocker Spaniel. A friendly and loyal family dog, the Schnocker may be less active than some of the other Miniature Schnauzer mixes. In fact, the Schnocker is a great lap dog. Schnockers love attention and thrive on the being in the middle of it, so much so that they are prone to separation anxiety. When company comes over, your Schnocker will soak up all the attention and may get so excited, that he has a tinkle accident. Just try to keep him from being overstimulated, and this should prevent accidents.

We have only touched on a few of the more popular Miniature Schnauzer designer mixes in this chapter. There are certainly more combinations out there, as breeders recognize the favorable qualities of the Mini Schnauzer breed, and attempt to bring those traits out in mixed puppies.

CHAPTER 16

How Do I Care for My Aging Miniature Schnauzer?

The average Miniature Schnauzer life expectancy is between 12 and 15 years, but the dog begins to show signs of aging at around 9 years of age. The aging process means changes for your older Miniature Schnauzer. You should be aware of the changes your Mini Schnauzer is experiencing so you can attend to his needs and keep him as healthy, fit, and active as possible. In this chapter, we will explain some of the conditions that may affect your Miniature Schnauzer has he enters his golden years.

*Older Miniature Schnauzers still need
exercise to keep them active and healthy.*

Appetite Changes

As your Mini Schnauzer ages, expect to see some changes in
his eating habits. He will probably eat less, and he may have a
harder time digesting his food. To make sure that he is getting
all the nutrients he needs, you may want to switch his food to
a senior formula. Discuss your Miniature Schnauzer's dietary
needs with your veterinarian or pet nutritionist to find the best
food for your aging Schnauzer. Take care when you switch your
dog's food, though. The change in diet may cause digestive
issues and add to the decrease in nutrient absorption that he
may already be experiencing. You should also be on the lookout

for rank-smelling breath, vomiting, or bleeding gums as these are all signs of digestive issues.

Water Consumption, Kidney Function, and Bladder Leakage

You may notice that your older Miniature Schnauzer is drinking more water. This could be due to a decrease in kidney function or diabetes, both common in aging dogs. With an increase in water consumption comes an increase in urination and the possibility of your dog having accidents in the house. Incontinence is more common in female dogs that have been spayed and is related to a decline in estrogen production. The decrease of estrogen causes a loss of muscle tone in the bladder. You may notice that your Mini Schnauzer leaks a little when she is asleep or resting. This is related to the loss of muscle control. Your dog is not being naughty…she may not be able to hold her bladder for as long as she could when she was younger.

As frustrating as you may find this, avoid punishing your dog. Whether male or female, your older Mini Schnauzer is not doing it to be bad. You may help him by letting him outside to do his business more often, or by putting down puppy pads. If your Miniature Schnauzer is experiencing bladder control issues, you should take him to your veterinarian for a check-up to rule out any serious complications.

Joint Pain and Stiffness

Dogs also experience joint pain and stiffness, just like their human counterparts, as they get older. Arthritis is not uncommon in older Miniature Schnauzers. You may notice that your older

Schnauzer is slower to get up the in the morning or after a long nap. Does he seem to be in any pain or discomfort? If you believe your Mini Schnauzer is having joint pain, schedule a veterinarian visit. Your veterinarian can prescribe arthritis medication to help ease your dog's pain.

The Miniature Schnauzer is a pleaser, so he may still play ball with you or join you on a jog, but keep in mind that he may not know his own limits. Some of the activities that he loved as a younger dog may now be too much for him to handle. You may notice that he seems fine during a run or during strenuous exercise, but that his recovery time is much longer. He is definitely feeling his age. Instead, you should consciously reduce the length of his walks or the number of times you toss the ball to him. Give him plenty of breaks and stop the exercise if he shows signs of fatigue or discomfort. If your Miniature Schnauzer has been your long time jogging buddy, watch for changes in his gait or for labored breathing.

Oftentimes, the first indication of joint pain and limited mobility in your Miniature Schnauzer is observed in the home. A dog who is used to laying on the couch or sleeping in his owner's bed may have a hard time jumping up to these places. Your little fella may act like he wants to jump up on the bed, but he doesn't follow through. This could be because his hips hurt or that he is now unsteady. Don't pat the bed encouragingly and call your dog up. He may fall and injure himself. Instead, lift him up. But remember that what goes up, must come down. Your Mini Schnauzer may also need your assistance in getting down from the bed or couch. Some dog owners will purchase a ramp, available at many pet stores, so the senior dog can safely climb up and down from the bed without hurting himself.

Change in Disposition

You may notice a personality change in your older Miniature Schnauzer. He may become cranky and less tolerant. Many humans experience the same sort of temperament changes as they get older…it is a normal part of the aging process. Knowing this, you should take steps to reduce stress and triggers for your dog, so he is as comfortable as can be. Watch your Mini Schnauzer around strangers and children. He may have been tolerant and friendly during his younger years, but he may be snappish as a senior dog. Avoid putting him in unfamiliar situations because you do not know how he will react.

Vision and Hearing Problems

Some Miniature Schnauzers experience hearing loss and sight loss as they age and may become completely blind or deaf. If you believe that your dog's sight or hearing is declining, you should take him to the veterinarian to rule out a more serious condition and to discuss treatment options. There may be ways to treat the condition or to, at the very least, slow the progression. Even if your dog becomes blind or deaf, he can still lead a normal life. You will just have to be a bit more diligent with his care. For example, if your Miniature Schnauzer is blind, try to keep his surroundings the same. Don't rearrange the furniture on him! Keep him on a leash when you are outside unless you have a fenced-in yard. Verbally warn your dog when a person or another dog is approaching. If your Mini Schnauzer is startled, he may react aggressively. If he has hearing loss, your dog may not hear your commands and warnings. He may be unaware of the danger and unable to hear you calling to him. Take steps to ensure that he isn't put in a situation that requires him to hear your commands.

Memory Loss

A sad, yet common, part of the aging process is memory loss. For your Miniature Schnauzer, this may mean that he ignores some of your commands. Chances are he is not stubborn or defiant... he just doesn't remember what he is supposed to do. Try to keep the commands simple and limited during his golden years. Don't expect him to be able to recall his whole repertoire of tricks. But do reward him with attention and treats, so he continues to connect the commands with positive reinforcement. Even with his memory loss, your little Mini Schnauzer still wants to please you and will try his best to do what you ask. If he doesn't get it right, don't punish him. Remember that it isn't his fault if he has some degree of memory loss.

Keep in mind that, in most cases, your Mini Schnauzer has spent his entire life with you, and has been a faithful and loyal and loving companion. We owe it to him to make his golden years a time of love and relaxation. He may need a bit more attention and a few more veterinarian visits, but you can enhance his later years and extend the quality of his life. It is the least we can do for our best friend.

CHAPTER 17

Conclusion

There is a reason why the Miniature Schnauzer is one of the most popular breeds of dog around the world. Smart, plucky, and energetic, the Mini Schnauzer packs a big personality into a small, compact body. His comical mustache and friendly demeanor will attract a lot of attention when you take your Miniature Schnauzer for walks. At home, your lovable Mini Schnauzer will follow you from room to room, and may even cuddle with you on the couch if the mood hits him.

Miniature Schnauzers are silly, boisterous, and outgoing.

Miniature Schnauzers can be quite vocal and territorial. He will alert you to approaching strangers, and anything else he thinks may be a threat to you…the mailman, passing jogger, or random squirrels. Don't worry, though. The Mini Schnauzer is highly trainable and quickly learns how to behave.

In general, Mini Schnauzers are a healthy breed with few breed-specific health issues, but you should always make sure to purchase your Miniature Schnauzer from a responsible breeder. This way, you reduce the chances of having a dog with chronic health problems. You can also keep your Mini Schnauzer in top form by following your veterinarian's recommendations for vaccinations, regular checkups, and diet.

The Miniature Schnauzer has a noble heritage. Bred as a diminutive of the much-admired German Standard Schnauzer, the Mini Schnauzer may have started as a ratting dog, working on the farms of rural Germany, but he has traded in his working life for the life of a companion dog. Although he still loves the wide open space of a farm, he is highly adaptable and can easily adjust to life in a big-city apartment.

Your Mini Schnauzer will thrive on attention and love, and will quickly become an important part of your family. Owning a Miniature Schnauzer means lots of laughter and lots of responsibility, and you will love every minute of it.

Your Trusted Miniature Schnauzer Resource List

If you are looking for additional information about Miniature Schnauzers and resources to help you find a reputable breeder in your region, here is a list of breeders and rescue organizations by location. This list should serve as a starting point for your journey to find your new best friend…your new Miniature Schnauzer.

Miniature Schnauzer Breeders in the United States

- Riggs Miniature Schnauzers
  http://www.ilovemyminiSchnauzer.com/
  Montpelier, Indiana
- Reberstein's Miniature Schnauzers
  http://www.loveSchnauzers.com/
  Brandon, Florida
- My Schnauzer Babies Miniature Schnauzers
  http://mySchnauzerbabies.com/
  Dunnellon, Florida
- Heavenly Miniature Schnauzers
  http://www.heavenlyminiatureSchnauzer.com/
  Grant's Pass, Oregon

- Skansen Kennel
  http://www.skansen.com/
  Sebastopol, California
- Rice's Miniature Schnauzers
  http://rices-minis.com/
  Lucasville, Ohio
- Blythewood Kennel
  http://www.blythewoodSchnauzers.com/
  Green Lane, Pennsylvania
- Attaway Miniature Schnauzers
  http://miniSchnauzers.com/
  Church Road, Virginia
- Family Schnauzer Babies
  http://familySchnauzerbabies.webs.com/about-us
  Melrose, Wisconsin
- McDorable Miniature Schnauzers
  http://mcdorable.com/
  Hartselle, Alabama
- ZakFive Kennel
  http://zacfivekennel.com/
  Hope, Arkansas
- Knotty Oak Ranch
  https://www.knottyoaks.com/
  Brownsville, New Jersey

- Spoiled Rotten Schnauzers
  http://www.spoiledrottenSchnauzers.com/
  Orem, Utah

Miniature Schnauzer Breeders in Canada

- Minutemen Miniature Schnauzers
  http://www.katewerk.com/minuteman.html
  Delisle, Saskatchewan
- Ebonylyn Schnauzers
  http://ebonylynSchnauzers.com/
  Ottawa, Ontario
- My Schnauzers
  http://www.bettsenterprises.com/
  Abbotsford, British Columbia
- Island Miniature Schnauzers
  http://toyminiatureSchnauzers.com/
  Sooke, British Columbia
- Silvercastle Miniature Schnauzers
  http://www.silvercastle.ca/
  St. Williams, Ontario
- Paw-Zazz Kennel
  http://www.paw-zazzkennel.com/
  Manotick, Ontario
- Nanny's Kennel
  http://www.nannyskennel.com/
  Ajax, Ontario

- Puppies on the Bridge
  http://www.puppiesonthebridge.com/
  Woodbridge, Ontario
- Ellite Miniature Schnauzers
  http://www.elliteminiatureSchnauzer.com/
  Owen Sound, Ontario
- Evalill Miniature Schnauzers
  http://www.evalillkennels.com/
  Milton, Ontario
- Sandy Shore Kennels
  http://www.sandyshorekennels.com/
  Shelburne County, Nova Scotia

Miniature Schnauzer Breeders in the U.K.

- Ferncliffe Schnauzers
  http://www.ferncliffeSchnauzers.com/
  Morecambe, Lancaster, England
- Holmchappell
  https://www.jessicaholm.co.uk/
  Shepton Mallet, Somerset, England
- LilySall Miniature Schnauzers
  http://www.lilysall.co.uk/
  West Yorkshire, England
- Tialexi Miniature Schnauzer
  http://www.tialexi.co.uk/
  Burnley, Lancaster, England

- RisePark Miniature Schnauzers
  http://www.risepark.co.uk/
  Solihull, West Midlands, England

Miniature Schnauzer Rescue Groups in the United States

- The American Miniature Schnauzer Club
  http://www.amsc.us/rescue/
- Schnauzer Rescue Me
  http://Schnauzer.rescueme.org
- Schnauzer Love Rescue
  https://Schnauzerloverescue.net/2015/
  serving Alabama, Georgia, Mississippi, Tennessee, Florida,
  South Carolina
- Arizona Schnauzer Rescue, Inc
  http://www.azSchnauzer.org/
  Serving Arizona
- Miniature Schnauzer Club of Northern California
  http://www.mscnc.us/
  Serving California
- New Jersey Schnauzer Rescue Network, Inc.
  http://www.njsrn.org/
  Serving New Jersey, Connecticut, Delaware, and Rhode Island
- Schnauzer Rescue of Mid-Atlantic
  http://www.Schnauzerrescue.net/
  Serving Delaware and Maryland

- Maple Creek Miniature Schnauzer Rescue
  https://www.maplecreekmsr.org/
  Serving Idaho, Washington, and Oregon
- Miniature Schnauzer Rescue of Illinois and the Midwest
  http://www.Schnauzerrescue.com/
  Serving Illinois, Iowa, Wisconsin
- Schnauzer Friends Rescue and Adoption
  http://www.sfra.net/
  Serving Kentucky
- Minneapolis St. Paul Miniature Schnauzer Rescue
  http://www.mspmsr.org/
  Serving Minnesota
- Boxer Schnauzer Rescue of the Ozarks
  http://bsro.org/
  Serving Missouri
- Schnauzer Rescue of the Carolinas
  http://www.Schnauzerrescueofthecarolinas.org/
  Serving North Carolina and South Carolina
- Miniature Schnauzer Rescue of Houston
  https://www.msrh.org/
  Serving Texas

Miniature Schnauzer Rescue Groups in Canada

*   Schnauzer Rescue Me
    http://Schnauzer.rescueme.org/ca

Miniature Schnauzer Rescue Groups in the U.K.

*   U.K. Schnauzer Rescue
    http://www.max-the-Schnauzer.com/uk-Schnauzer-rescue.html